Kenneth D. Barney

FREEDOM: A GUARANTEE FOR EVERYBODY

Adapted from *Romans* by G. Raymond Carlson

Gospel Publishing House
Springfield, Missouri
02-0891

FREEDOM: A GUARANTEE FOR EVERYBODY
© 1975 by the Gospel Publishing House
Springfield, Missouri 65802
Adapted from Romans by G. Raymond Carlson © 1962 by the
Gospel Publishing House. All rights reserved.
Library of Congress Catalog Card Number: 75-34644
ISBN 0-88243-891-3
Printed in the United States of America

**A teacher's guide for individual or group study with this book
is available from the Gospel Publishing House.**

Contents

ONE

A Preacher Writes a Letter

"PAUL, A SERVANT OF JESUS CHRIST." There was no egotism in this man. He was an apostle, a great preacher, a highly educated ex-Pharisee. But what mattered most to Paul was that he was Christ's servant.

After calling himself a servant, he declared the office in which Christ had placed him. He was made an apostle by divine decree. Today he might call himself an ambassador. An apostle is one who is sent on a mission.

Two words picture Paul's career: "called" and "separated." He was called to apostleship. Always he realized he was a separated man. He had a special work to do. For this task he was separated. This does not mean he became a hermit. He mingled with people, but lived apart from personal ambitions. Life to Paul was a commitment, a commission, and a consecration.

Thus the author of Romans opens his letter with the greeting, "Paul, a servant of Jesus Christ, called to be an apostle, separated unto the gospel of God" (Romans 1:1).

If you have read the Book of Acts you know the background of this man. The last thing he expected to

5

be was a preacher of the gospel of Christ. He had been a hater of that message. Talk about sincerity! No more sincere person ever lived. Before his conversion Paul believed that the Christian church must be stamped out. He considered it an insult to the religion of his ancestors. The very name of Jesus enraged him. He was determined to eliminate its influence completely.

On the road to Damascus all of that changed. Paul (then called Saul) was hurrying to the city to arrest as many Christians as possible. He had already been a spectator at the death of the first Christian martyr, Stephen. Perhaps the radiance of Stephen's face became unbearable to Paul's conscience. It may have contributed to his unusual drive in harassing the Christians.

Paul told the story over and over during his ministry. Always it was the plain simple facts. He had been blinded by a light from heaven. He had fallen to the ground and heard the voice of Jesus saying, "Saul, Saul, why persecutest thou Me?" From that moment the persecutor became the gospel's greatest champion.

The Message

"Paul, a servant of Jesus Christ, called to be an apostle, separated unto the gospel of God (which he had promised afore by his prophets in the holy Scriptures,) concerning his Son Jesus Christ our Lord, which was made of the seed of David according to the flesh, and declared to be the Son of God with power, according to the Spirit of holiness, by the resurrection from the dead: by whom we have received grace and apostleship, for obedience to the faith among all nations, for his name: among whom are ye also the called of Jesus Christ" (Romans 1:1-6).

Paul's message is the gospel. The word *gospel* is a favorite with him. It means "good news."

The gospel unfolds in the New Testament, but its shadows are clearly seen in the Old Testament. During the centuries before Jesus came, God prepared the world for the work He would do. In fulfillment of the divine promise the gospel came at the appointed time as "promised afore by his prophets in the holy Scriptures." The promise became a reality in the person of Jesus Christ. He is the center of the gospel. Without Him there is *no* gospel.

When Paul says that Jesus was made of the seed of David according to the flesh he is referring to His virgin birth; His incarnation. This was the great miracle by which He became man. He entered the stream of human history supernaturally. His life did not begin at Bethlehem. He is from all eternity, for He is the second person of the Godhead. On that first Christmas Eve it was only His earthly life that began.

Jesus was not only a man. He was "declared to be the Son of God with power." And this power was displayed in His resurrection. An ambassador carries credentials when he goes abroad to represent his country. Christ's credentials are His resurrection. This is all the proof we need that He is the Son of God.

What power was manifested in that resurrection! Satan held the power of death in his hands until then. But Jesus wrested all of the devil's authority from him. The resurrection is to the gospel what the foundation is to a house. If Jesus had not risen there would have been no gospel to preach. There would have been memories of a good man, but a good man does not have the power to redeem other men from sin.

7

Notice, in verse six, that Paul told the Romans they were also "the called of Jesus Christ." An apostle had no "corner" on the gospel. Everyone who responds to the message by accepting Christ is also called.

THE AUDIENCE

"To all that be in Rome, beloved of God, called to be saints: Grace to you and peace from God our Father, and the Lord Jesus Christ. First, I thank my God through Jesus Christ for you all, that your faith is spoken of throughout the whole world. For God is my witness, whom I serve with my spirit in the gospel of his Son, that without ceasing I make mention of you always in my prayers" (Romans 1:7-9).

The "all that be in Rome" does not include the whole population. It was to those "beloved of God, called to be saints." They were literally "God's loved ones."

Some may misunderstand the meaning of the word *saint*. It is not the church which decides who are saints. Every Christian is a saint. He becomes one when he accepts Christ. It is not because of some great thing he has done, but through the grace of God that saved him from sin.

Wouldn't it be inspiring to get a letter that began by wishing you "grace and peace"? Please note the order: Grace comes first; then peace. There is no way to enjoy peace with God unless you have accepted His grace in Christ. Grace is God's unmerited favor. It is not earned. It *cannot* be.

The Roman church was not founded by any apostle. Yet their faith was spoken of throughout the world. Wherever Paul went he heard of these Christians. God is pleased when a church is known by its faith.

8

This is more important than its numbers or financial report. Without faith it is impossible to please God (Hebrews 11:6). In the midst of Rome's might and glory, God's people were men and women of faith.

Rome was a wicked city. It was full of idolaters. The chief object of worship was the emperor himself. But right in such surroundings God had a people. It is the glory of the gospel that it enables men to live clean lives in dirty surroundings.

It must have been thrilling for those Roman saints to hear that such a man as Paul prayed for them continually. Sometimes a friend may say, "I'm praying for you," but later forget his promise. Not so with Paul. He must have had a long prayer list. No doubt those prayers sustained God's people throughout the world. Prayer was the key to Paul's spiritual power. It is the only key to such power for anyone.

Paul had not met these people. But so many reports about them had reached his ears that he felt he must let them know how much he was concerned about them.

THE PURPOSE

"Making request, if by any means now at length I might have a prosperous journey by the will of God to come unto you. For I long to see you, that I may impart unto you some spiritual gift, to the end ye may be established; that is, that I may be comforted together with you by the mutual faith both of you and me. Now I would not have you ignorant, brethren, that oftentimes I purposed to come unto you, (but was let hitherto), that I might have some fruit among you also, even as among other Gentiles. I am debtor both to the Greeks, and to the Barbarians, both to the wise and to the unwise. So, as much as

9

in me is, I am ready to preach the gospel to you that are at Rome also" (Romans 1:10-15).

As much as Paul wanted to visit Rome he was anxious that when the trip was made it would be in the will of God. That will was always uppermost in his mind.

When Paul finally went to Rome it was as a prisoner. Yet he considered even this to be in the will of God. He was a committed man, and never referred to himself as Rome's prisoner, but as the prisoner of Jesus Christ. Paul practiced what he preached. In Romans 8:28 he declared that "all things," when put together, will be for our good if we love and serve God.

Paul's longing to visit Rome was for spiritual reasons. He wanted to establish the Roman Christians in the truths of the gospel.

The apostle considered himself a debtor. He was not interested in receiving, but in giving. Ever since his conversion he felt that he owed something. Whether he was preaching to the Greeks or barbarians, the wise or unwise, he considered it all part of discharging his debt.

"Not Ashamed"

"For I am not ashamed of the gospel of Christ, for it is the power of God unto salvation to everyone that believeth, to the Jew first, and also to the Greek. For therein is the righteousness of God revealed from faith to faith, as it is written, The just shall live by faith" (Romans 1:16,17).

These verses are the theme of the entire Book of Romans. Paul boldly declared, "I am not ashamed." No matter where he went he told about Christ. He spoke just as emphatically in the presence of kings as to men in the street. Christ is for everybody, and Paul was determined to *reach* everybody with the message. In a day when there were no mass media, he literally shook the world with the gospel of which he was not ashamed. He held back nothing from the Lord. His whole life was pointed in one direction.

THE BIGGEST WORD IN THE BIBLE

"Salvation!" No doubt about it, this is the biggest word in the Bible. The salvation of men's souls is the aim of the gospel. And it's to "every one." No wonder the apostle was not ashamed.

First of all, we are saved when we believe. "Thy faith hath saved thee" (Luke 7:50). Compare Acts 16:30,31; 1 Corinthians 1:18; 2 Corinthians 2:15; 2 Timothy 1:9. This belief releases the repentant sinner from the penalty and guilt of sin. The moment he believes, he is brought from his lost state, born of God, cleansed, set free from condemnation. He is clothed in the righteousness of Christ. This is called "justification."

But this is not the end. It is only the beginning. In a very true sense we *are* saved, we are *being saved*, and we *shall be* saved. After conversion we are being saved daily from the power and control of sin. This aspect of salvation is often called "sanctification." This is what Paul meant when he declared, "For the law of the Spirit of life in Christ Jesus hath made me free from the law of sin and death" (Romans 8:2). Compare Romans 6:14; 2 Corinthians 3:18; Galatians 2:20; 4:19; 5:16; Philippians 2:12,13.

The believer *shall be* saved when he is delivered from the *presence* of sin. This, of course, is when he reaches heaven. Compare Ephesians 5:25-27; Philippians 1:6; 1 Peter 1:3-5; 1 John 3:1,2. The Bible calls

11

this (glorification.) It is the ultimate result of salvation.

These three aspects of salvation (justification, sanctification, and glorification) are seen in the following Scriptures: 1 Corinthians 1:30; Ephesians 5:25-27; Philippians 1:6; 1 Thessalonians 1:9,10; Titus 2:11-13.

Man can contribute nothing to his salvation. He must believe. Salvation is a divine undertaking. Can anyone understand it? Not from a purely natural point of reasoning. It is beyond the comprehension of human minds. It is one of those things that can be experienced but not understood by the intellect. Salvation is a supernatural work.

The gospel is for all. It embraces everyone. God so loved "the world." He has no favorites. He is color-blind. One's nationality gives him no special advantages.

No wonder Paul used the word *power* when he talked about salvation. Our generation has seen many displays of power. But the power required to save a soul from eternal death makes all other power look insignificant.

How Do You Become a Saint?

The one condition attached to salvation is found in those words, "that believeth." That's all. Faith is the key.

True faith must be based on the Bible. It cannot rest on our feelings. They are too changeable. It's what the Word says that counts.

It is the believer's faith to which God responds. It is not his good works, long prayers, or good intentions.

Faith is necessary in both the spiritual and natural realms. The farmer exercises faith when he sows his

12

seed. The businessman must have faith when he invests in capital expansion. Were it not for faith the depositor would never leave his paycheck at the bank. We live our natural lives with this measure of faith. How much more should we believe the Word.

Faith is founded on hope, and hope is "desire with expectation of obtaining." (Compare Romans 8:24.) "As many as received him, to them gave he power to become the sons of God, even to them that believe on his name" (John 1:12).

Faith brings assurance. It involves the intellect, emotions, and will. It does more than influence our feelings. It gets hold of the steering wheel of our life, which is our will.

Note the decision of the Prodigal Son. He thought ("came to himself"); he felt ("I will arise"); he acted ("he arose and came to his father").

Martin Luther was sitting in his cell in Wittenberg, reading the Book of Romans. Coming to verse 17 he read, "The just shall live by faith." As he thought on those words joy flooded his heart. Up to that time he had tried to earn salvation, but always felt he had not yet done enough. Through this verse the Holy Spirit revealed to him that man is saved by faith, not works. Romans 1:17 became to him "the gate to Paradise." This was how the great reformer was converted.

A saint is one who has been made righteous by God because he has trusted in the righteousness of Christ. That righteousness becomes like clothing that God puts on him. His own righteousness is like a suit of clothes that has become dirty and ragged. God does more than patch up the old clothes. He gives the repenting, believing sinner a brand-new suit, and calls it "the righteousness of God."

13

TWO

God Goes to Court

"BUT GOD SHOWS HIS ANGER from heaven against all sinful, evil men who push away the truth from them. For the truth about God is known to them instinctively; God has put this knowledge in their hearts. Since earliest times men have seen the earth and sky and all God made, and have known of His existence and great eternal power. So they will have no excuse [when they stand before God at Judgment Day].

"Yes, they knew about Him all right, but they wouldn't admit it or worship him or even thank him for all his daily care. And after a while they began to think up silly ideas of what God was like and what he wanted them to do. The result was that their foolish minds became dark and confused. Claiming themselves to be wise without God, they became utter fools instead. And then, instead of worshiping the glorious, ever-living God, they took wood and stone and made idols for themselves, carving them to look like mere birds and animals and snakes and puny men.

"So God let them go ahead into every sort of sex sin, and do whatever they wanted to—yes, vile and

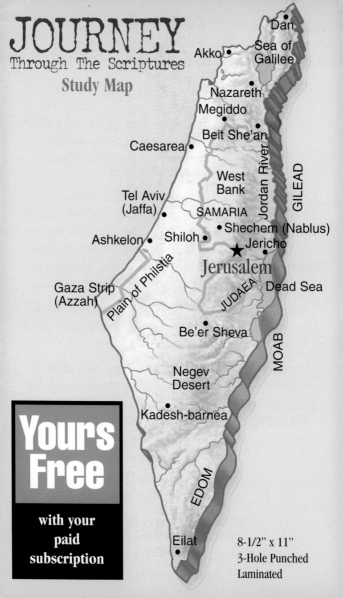

YOURS FREE . . .

with your paid subscription!

Continue your *Journey Through The Scriptures* with Rabbi Eckstein and *The Fellowship*, and you will receive this full-color map of Israel absolutely *free* with your paid subscription renewal order!

It is always important to have a map handy when you travel through the Bible—and this easy-to-read, detailed map of the Holy Land will add an exciting new dimension to your Bible study. With your new study map, you will be able to follow the lives of Bible character and pinpoint important biblical events as you read about them each month on your *Journey Through The Scriptures*!

Seeing the places where the Bible's great stories took place will help you put these events in their geographical context, and will aid you in understanding the Scripture.

This map is made of durable plastic and 3-hole punched, so you can keep it in your *Journey Through The Scriptures* binder! And best of all, it is *free* with your paid renewal order! **Mail the reply slip and your check today so you will be sure to receive your Israel study map!**

INTERNATIONAL FELLOWSHIP
OF CHRISTIANS AND JEWS

30 North LaSalle Street • Suite 2600
Chicago, IL 60602-3356
312-641-7200 • (FAX) 312-641-7201
www.ifcj.org • info@ifcj.org

sinful things with each other's bodies" (Romans 1:18-24, *Living Bible Paraphrased*).

"No excuse!" That's God's indictment of this human race. No alibis accepted! "You have known about Me through nature itself. Your rebellion is deliberate. My only choice is to pour out My wrath on you." This is what God thunders to the whole world.

The only way man can escape such judgment is to receive God's righteousness. By himself, man cannot attain righteousness. The Bible records man's repeated failures in trying to be good.

Romans 1:18 to Romans 3:20 is like a court scene. The whole world is declared guilty before God.

Sin established a process of degeneration. This process ends in judgment. When man forsook God, God forsook man. When man debased himself in idolatry, God gave him up to debasement in immorality. The expression, "God gave them up," appears in the King James Version three times in Chapter One. It's terrible when God takes off the brakes and lets a man go careening downward. But this is what persistent rebellion produces. It can end no other way.

GOD—ANGRY? REALLY?

All truth has two sides. The gospel is primarily the message of God's love. The whole Bible focuses on that love. It is so boundless that a mortal mind cannot grasp it. The miracle is that God does not just love people who love Him. He loves those who actually hate Him. He is continually trying to win them.

But there is another side. God could not be God if He allowed sin to go unpunished. It would be like repealing all of the laws in a city and never punishing anyone for anything. Anarchy and chaos would be

15

the quick result. God has created a universe based on laws. One of those laws is that whatsoever a man soweth that shall he also reap.

Alongside the Bible's teaching about divine love there is the ever-present truth of His wrath. God is not arbitrary. He is not peevish. The Bible constantly call Him "long-suffering." His love stretches far beyond what would be the breaking point for human love. He waits and waits and waits before He brings judgment down on a sinner's head.

But there does come a time when men go so far in the wrong direction that God has to act. Sin is like a horrible cancer that must finally be removed by the surgery of divine judgment.

WHEN GOD LETS GO

"Instead of believing what they knew was the truth about God, they deliberately chose to believe lies. So they prayed to the things God made, but wouldn't obey the blessed God who made these things.

"That is why God let go of them and let them do all these evil things, so that even their women turned against God's natural plan for them and indulged in sex sin with each other. And the men, instead of having a normal sex relationship with women, burned with lust for each other, men doing shameful things with other men and, as a result, getting paid within their own souls with the penalty they so richly deserved" (Romans 1:25-27, *Living Bible Paraphrased*).

Here Paul talks again about God letting people go. The King James Version says, "gave them up." Man is a free moral agent. As powerful as God is, He will not force anyone to do the right thing. If a man demonstrates long enough that he wants no part of God he will finally be allowed to have his way completely. The Lord withdraws all restraints and lets the rebel go full speed ahead to his doom.

Obviously Paul is discussing homosexuality in these verses. Adultery is an abuse of a normal appetite, but homosexuality is even more base, for it is perversion. You don't have to be told that this monster is lifting its ugly head in society today. In many quarters it is considered a light matter. But this is not the way God views it.

Before a man fights God he should be aware of the ultimate consequences. As long as the Lord is placing roadblocks in front of us there is still hope. While His restraints are upon us there is still time to escape the wrath to come. But the most fearful thing that can happen to a human being is to cross that unseen line where God finally lets go. From then on it's all downhill. The life slips faster and faster into degradation. It's full speed ahead! The man or woman to whom this happens may think he or she is having more fun than ever. One's spirit may even be light and free. There may be no sense of the awful condition into which he has entered. This ignorance makes the tragedy even worse.

We live in a permissive atmosphere today where it is not difficult to reach such a condition. The pressures of sin are tremendous. Satan will see to it that his slaves have little time to think. He lulls them to sleep on the opiates of pleasure, lust, security, and never-ending activity. Their awakening will be terrible.

Don't Fool With Truth!

All of this downward plunge starts, Paul says, when man deliberately chooses to believe lies instead of God's truth. The King James Version says, "who

17

changed the truth of God into a lie" (Romans 1:25).

Truth is God's lifeline to man. Jesus declared *himself* to be the Truth. All of God's truth is embodied in the person of His Son. The Bible reveals truth. The man who follows it is walking in a safe path.

But truth isn't pleasant to everyone. For one thing, it tells us that we are sinners. Proud people don't enjoy that kind of talk. Men want some kind of religion, but not everyone wants the true kind. So they invent religions of their own. Often these false teachings start out with a little truth. But eventually it becomes twisted to suit the individual's own ideas. It deteriorates into a convenient way for him to put his conscience to sleep.

Any lie is bad. But when it is produced by twisting and torturing truth it becomes all the more deadly.

In ancient times this changing of truth into a lie resulted in idolatry. Instead of worshiping God men looked at things God had made and worshiped them. No matter what form idolatry takes it always operates on the same principle. It brings God down to man's level. This is exactly the opposite to the way it should be. If man is to escape divine wrath he must be lifted up to *God's* level. This is why Jesus came to earth. He came to make it possible for man to receive God's righteousness and be saved.

Even before men reach eternity they pay a terrible price for tampering with truth. They get "paid within their own souls." The results of sin appear in their own lives. Their personalities are affected. Their minds are warped. Even their bodies feel the impact of such a way of life.

In our permissive times the teaching is widespread that truth is what every man makes it. There are no absolutes with many people today. But this is not what the Bible teaches. There is one truth; one way to heaven; one way to please God and be delivered from judgment. We come *His* way or lose our souls.

When liberals in the pulpit attack the Bible as being full of errors they are undermining truth. And they are preparing their listeners for disaster. They are destroying the only safe foundation on which a life can be built. And they provide no other foundation in its place. What a judgment awaits such false teachers!

"GET OUT OF HERE, GOD!"

"So it was that when they gave God up and would not even acknowledge him, God gave them up to doing everything their evil minds could think of. Their lives became full of every kind of wickedness and sin, of greed and hate, envy, murder, fighting, lying, bitterness, and gossip. They were backbiters, haters of God, insolent, proud braggarts, always thinking of new ways of sinning and continually being disobedient to their parents. They tried to misunderstand, broke their promises, and were heartless —without pity. They were fully aware of God's death penalty for these crimes, yet they went right ahead and did them anyway, and encouraged others to do them, too" (Romans 1:28-32, *Living Bible Paraphrased*).

This is exactly what Paul pictures men saying: "Get out of here, God!" So God granted their demand and "gave them up." They were given over to thinking thoughts, doing deeds, and living lives for which they were not created. Man was made in God's image and for His glory. How low he has fallen!

The last verses of this chapter are a catalog of sins that are the result of total depravity. When the apostle wrote these words they were a picture of the heathen world. But they are also a portrayal of the headlines of today's newspaper.

The climax is reached in verse 32. God's wrath has been revealed to man; yet man ignores it. He goes all out in sin, revels in it, boasts about it, and has pleasure in others that do the same. This is the climax of sin. Man can sink no lower!

This terrible picture of the human heart is not pretty. We don't like it. In fact it is nauseating. But it is true. God has drawn the picture. Man may deny it; he may try to evade it. But it is life as lived by the sinner.

This passage establishes responsibility for sin. That responsibility is in proportion to the light an individual has, however small that light may be. Man is guilty and without excuse.

These verses also emphasize the certainty of punishment. It is inevitable. The wrath of God is "revealed." In the midst of it all, of course, His mercy still shines brightly. He must condemn and punish all who continue in their rebellion. But at the same time He stands ready to forgive the one who repents and turns to Christ. If men go to hell they must crash through the roadblock of the Cross. They must trample the precious blood of Jesus underfoot. They must brush aside the pleadings of the Holy Spirit.

The Snare of Self-Righteousness

" 'Well,' you may be saying, 'What terrible people you have been talking about!' But wait a minute! You are just as bad. When you say they are wicked and should be punished, you are talking about yourselves, for you do these very same things" (Romans 2:1, *Living Bible Paraphrased*).

Then, as now, self-righteousness was a trap that swallowed up many. Paul is explaining the universality of sin. He declares the moral degradation of the whole human family. Men went so low that "God gave them up." Self-righteous folks plead, "Not guilty." They point to their morality. They say, "Those people may do terrible things, but I don't!"

The Pharisee pictured in Luke 18:9-14 is an example of the self-righteous moralist. The publican portrays the degraded sinner. The latter repented. The Pharisee prayed "within himself." But his prayers went no higher than the ceiling. Condemning others he said, "God, I thank thee that I am not as other men are." What happened when it was all over? The publican "went down to his house justified." The Pharisee went home still a sinner.

The self-righteous man makes these fatal mistakes. First, he has no conception of the righteousness of God. He tries to think of holiness in human terms. He compares himself with other *men* instead of with God.

Second, the self-righteous individual does not fully understand man's utter sinfulness. He condemns those whose sin is glaring and notorious. But he justifies himself because his sins are not so apparent. He thinks in terms of big sins and little sins; black sins and white ones. He sees his good deeds being weighed on God's scales and overbalancing any sins he may commit.

The self-righteous man sees only *outward* sins. He does not realize that God continually looks at the heart. It completely escapes his attention that there are hidden sins in man's spirits that are just as poisonous as the outward ones. He can easily call adultery a sin, but does not realize impure thoughts condemn

21

a man before God also. He sees murder as a violation of God's law, but does not comprehend that his hate is a vicious sin that brings divine wrath down upon him.

"I am respectable. I am cultured. I am refined. Surely God will not condemn me!" These are the thoughts of the self-righteous fellow. But they are erroneous. Such a concept is totally false in the eyes of a holy God. Judgment Day is going to be full of surprises to both modern and ancient Pharisees.

JUDGMENT!

"And we know that God, in justice, will punish anyone who does such things as these. Do you think that God will judge and condemn others for doing them and overlook you when you do them, too? Don't you realize how patient he is being with you? Or don't you care? Can't you see that he has been waiting all this time without punishing you, to give you time to turn from your sin? His kindness is meant to lead you to repentance.

"But no, you won't listen; and so you are saving up terrible punishment for yourselves because of your stubbornness in refusing to turn from your sin; for there is going to come a day of wrath when God will be the just Judge of all the world. He will give each one whatever his deeds deserve. He will give eternal life to those who patiently do the will of God, seeking for the unseen glory and honor and eternal life that he offers. But he will terribly punish those who fight against the truth of God and walk in evil ways—God's anger will be poured out upon them. There will be sorrow and suffering for Jews and Gentiles alike who keep on sinning. But there will be glory and honor and peace from God for all who obey him, whether they are Jews or Gentiles. For God treats everyone the same.

"He will punish sin wherever it is found. He will punish the heathen when they sin, even though they never had God's written laws, for down in their hearts they know right from wrong. God's laws are written within them; their own conscience accuses them, or sometimes excuses them. And God will punish the Jews for sinning because they have his written laws but don't obey them. They know what is right but don't do it. After all, salvation is not given to those who know what to do, unless they do it. The day will surely come when at God's command Jesus Christ will judge the secret lives of everyone, their inmost thoughts and motives; this is all part of God's great plan which I proclaim" (Romans 2:2-16, *Living Bible Paraphrased*).

The first principle of God's judgment is justice "according to truth," as the King James Version has it. Man may judge on the basis of partial knowledge, but God has all the facts. God does not love to judge. He is not willing that any should perish (2 Peter 3:9). In fact, these chapters in Romans are written with a view to bringing man to God's grace as revealed in Christ. Man's treatment of the Lord Jesus is the focal point of the whole process: Accept Christ and receive God's righteousness and deliverance. Reject Christ and face the devastating judgment of which God has warned.

THREE

An Appeal That Falls Flat

"YOU JEWS THINK ALL IS WELL between yourselves and God because he gave his laws to you; you brag that you are his special friends. Yes, you know what he wants; you know right from wrong and favor the right because you have been taught his laws from earliest youth. You are so sure of the way to God that you could point it out to a blind man. You think of yourselves as beacon lights, directing men who are lost in darkness to God. You think that you can guide the simple and teach even children the affairs of God, for you really know his laws, which are full of all knowledge and truth" (Romans 2:17-20, *Living Bible Paraphrased*).

Paul is arraigning the Jew. The Pharisaical Jews of that day were probably the most self-righteous people of all time. Who, better than Paul, could strike at their self-righteousness? He had been one of them. But on the Damascus road he found his mistake. From then on he knew that righteousness was not obtained by keeping the Law.

We are still in a courtroom scene. Here the self-righteous, religious boaster is stripped of his cloak of imagined righteousness. The Jew was the "religious" man of that day. He was proud and self-sufficient.

He gloried in knowing the Law. He considered himself above the Gentile spiritually.

The Jew had the Law, but the Law didn't have him. The very thing in which he rested condemned him unless he could keep it—which, of course, he could not. Jesus alone kept the Law, and the Jews rejected Him (Galatians 3:10-13).

The fact that the Jew knew the will of God only increased his condemnation. When he sinned it was against spiritual light. His knowledge of God, unfortunately, was only a head knowledge. And he has always had plenty of company—even to this present hour!

The Jew of Paul's day was a picture of being religious without being redeemed. Such a statement shocks some people, but it is as true as ever. No amount of rule-keeping saves the soul. Religious ritual is of no avail. All of this only makes the sinner more guilty.

Clean Hands and a Dirty Heart

"Yes, you teach others—then why don't you teach yourselves? You tell others not to steal—do *you* steal? You say it is wrong to commit adultery—do *you* do it? You say, 'Don't pray to idols,' and then make money your god instead.

"You are so proud of knowing God's laws, *but you dishonor him by breaking them.* No wonder the Scriptures say that the world speaks evil of God because of you.

"Being a Jew is worth something if you obey God's laws, but if you don't then you are no better off than the heathen. And if the heathen obey God's laws, won't God give them all the rights and honors he planned to give the Jews? In fact, those heathen will be much better off than you Jews who know so much about God and have his promises but don't obey his laws.

"For you are not real Jews just because you were born of Jewish parents or because you have gone through the Jewish initiation ceremony of circumcision. No, a real Jew is anyone whose heart is right with God. For God is not looking for those who cut their bodies in actual body circumcision, but He is looking for those with changed hearts and minds. Whoever has that kind of change in his life will get his praise from God, even if not from you" (Romans 2:21-29, *Living Bible Paraphrased*).

James instructs us to be "doers of the Word" (James 1:22). Paul questions the Jew about his doing, and the Jew can only plead guilty.

The force of the apostle's indictment was that these people were very careful about outward ceremonies, but negligent about their hearts. They had clean hands, but dirty hearts. How often they washed themselves with water as they observed their strict ritual. This removed outward dirt. But it left the inside of them untouched.

Although these remarks are directed to the Jew, they should jolt everyone who professes to be a Christian. Do we merely pay lip service to the truth? Is there a difference between the actual standards we live by and what we claim?

Paul points to the contrast between the Jew "outwardly" and the Jew "inwardly." He declares that the ordinance of circumcision was useless without personal righteousness. True circumcision, he says, is the cleansing of the heart. Outward ceremonies will not save the soul. This includes water baptism and Communion, which have great spiritual significance but are only empty forms if there has been no change of heart.

GOD FORBID!

"Then what's the use of being a Jew? Are there any special benefits for them from God? Is there any value in the Jewish circumcision ceremony? Yes, being a Jew has many advantages.

"First of all, God trusted them with His laws [so that they could know and do his will]. True, some of them were unfaithful, but just because they broke their promises to God, does that mean God will break his promises? Of course not! Though everyone else in the world is a liar, God is not. Do you remember what the Book of Psalms says about this? That God's words will always prove true and right, no matter who questions them.

"'But,' some say, 'our breaking faith with God is good, our sins serve a good purpose, for people will notice how good God is when they see how bad we are. Is it fair, then, for him to punish us when our sins are helping him?' (That is the way some people talk.) God forbid! Then what kind of God would he be, to overlook sin? How could he ever condemn anyone? For he could not judge and condemn me as a sinner if my dishonesty brought him glory by pointing up his honesty in contrast to my lies. If you follow through with that idea you come to this: the worse we are, the better God likes it! But the damnation of those who say such things is just. Yet some claim that this is what I preach!" (Romans 3:1-8, *Living Bible Paraphrased*).

Paul freely admits the Jew had an advantage because God's laws were given to him. Tragically this worked to his condemnation because he did not, and could not, *keep* those laws.

It should be remembered that the Jew is not cast away. He is set aside. During the present age God is calling out a church that is largely Gentile. When the age ends at the return of the Lord the attention of God will be turned to Israel again.

Paul was obviously indignant at the argument he had heard from some—that the more sinful a man is, the more it glorifies the holy character of God. This twisted reasoning led to the conclusion that God could not justly punish a man for sin because that sin only brought more glory to Him. "Preposterous.," Paul cried. "God forbid!" People who say such things are guilty of abusing the mercy of God.

The condemnation of the Jew who had such spiritual privileges but lost them is a warning to everyone —Jew or Gentile. Rather than boasting about spiritual advantages we should be sure we are using them and not wasting them.

No Exceptions

"Well, then, are we Jews *better* than others? No, not at all, for we have already shown that all men alike are sinners, whether Jews or Gentiles" (Romans 3:9, *Living Bible Paraphrased*).

The question of unrighteousness among Gentiles and Jews has been fully considered. *Both* are unrighteous. Now Paul proves that both are guilty. They are under the dominion of sin. The condemnation of God is upon them. Man is a sinner by nature. He is a sinner by deliberate choice. He is a sinner in God's sight. All men are under sin, and God will deal with them accordingly. There is not one single exception.

No one likes to say, "I'm wrong." Everyone likes to point to someone he considers worse than himself. How often have you heard the cry, "I'm just as good as that fellow. And he professes to be a Christian!" This carries no weight with God. It adds nothing to a sinner's plea for acquittal. Someone else's crime doesn't make ours any less.

Even Adam tried to blame Eve for his disobedience. Passing the buck is a favorite human pastime. Today "society" gets the blame for just about everything. People try to excuse themselves because of their environment or heredity. "Sin" is an unpopular word. But it's in God's vocabulary, and there is no point in ignoring it. It won't go away.

Paul declared that Jews and Gentiles are on the same footing before God. They are all declared sinful. No one can claim special privileges. Americans may sometimes imagine themselves to have a special advantage spiritually because theirs is a so-called "Christian nation." Nothing could be farther from the truth. An American is a sinner and so is the Muslim or Buddhist or fetish worshiper. God has no pets. Nationality doesn't enter the picture. The affluent man is a sinner, and so is the poor man.

Everyone would like to think that in some way he can escape the universal condemnation. Paul levels a heavy barrage at the Jews because they were "religious" people. How many sermons have you heard about "the good moral man"? He is probably harder to reach than the drunkard in the gutter. Self-righteousness is a cloak people do not want to part with. But the sooner we shed the cloak the better off we shall be.

THE JUDGE LOWERS THE BOOM

"As the Scriptures say,

" 'No one is good—no one in all the world is innocent.'

"No one has ever really followed God's paths, or even truly wanted to.

"Every one has turned away; all have gone wrong. No one anywhere has kept on doing what is right; not one.

"Their talk is foul and filthy like the stench from an open grave. Their tongues are loaded with lies. Everything they say has in it the sting and poison of deadly snakes.

"Their mouths are full of cursing and bitterness.

"They are quick to kill, hating anyone who disagrees with them.

"Wherever they go they leave misery and trouble behind them, and they have never known what it is to feel secure or enjoy God's blessing.

"They care nothing about God nor what He thinks of them" (Romans 3:10-18), *Living Bible Paraphrased*).

Listen to those sweeping charges of guilt! No one is good. No one is innocent. No one follows God or wants to. Everyone has turned away. All have gone wrong. No one does right.

In this passage God is like a doctor, diagnosing the deadly spiritual ailments of the human race. He minces no words. He does not try to make something pretty which is ugly. Sin is a filthy, degraded picture.

If a preacher said things like this about people from the pulpit they would want to run him out of town. But this is *God* speaking! He is telling it "like it is." There is nothing good about anyone, He declares.

What's the use of telling someone he only has indigestion when he really has cancer? God is not being cruel with this diagnosis; He is being merciful. No one is going to submit to treatment if he doesn't think he is sick. So God proceeds to tell the whole human race just how sick it is.

The human heart is desperately wicked. It is totally depraved. These verses are a photograph of human nature in its fallen and unredeemed state. Man did not begin on the bottom of the ladder and start a long climb upward, as the evolutionists say. He began in the image of God and fell. Ever since, he has slipped farther and farther into this slimy pit of sin. His own works cannot get him out. Nothing but the gospel can. But before man will listen to a message of salvation he has to know for sure that he is completely lost.

THE ACCUSED STANDS SILENT

"So the judgment of God lies very heavily upon the Jews, for they are responsible to keep God's laws instead of doing all these evil things; not one of them has any excuse; in fact, all the world stands hushed and guilty before Almighty God.

"Now do you see it? No one can ever be made right in God's sight by doing what the Law commands. For the more we know of God's laws, the clearer it becomes that we aren't obeying them; his laws serve only to make us see that we are sinners" (Romans 3: 19,20, *Living Bible Paraphrased*).

The courtroom scene comes to a close. The trial is over. A strong, yet simple, statement of the court's findings is given. These verses render the verdict. All are guilty and lost through sin.

The accused stands defenseless. He has heard the charges of the prosecution and cannot answer them. He knows he is guilty, and there is nothing to say.

No man will escape God's maximum sentence. The wages of sin is death—*eternal* death (Romans 6:23).

Two expressions, "before Almighty God" (v. 19), and "in God's sight" (v. 20) are significant. It is not a case of what other men think. It is how an individual appears before God that counts.

The Law did its work, but it could not justify. It could only condemn. But, thank God, there came to the world one day a sinless One who kept the Law perfectly. It was God's Son, the Lord Jesus Christ. By trusting in Him and receiving His salvation the guilty sinner can be declared righteous in God's sight.

Christianity is not man's search for God. It is God's search for sinful man. The Bible does not record man's search. It is God's message of redemption. Sin has done its work. Man is guilty before God. There is no hope for him outside of divine grace. Salvation can never come through the Law. What man needs is some kind of good news. Is there such news? Yes. It is called "the gospel." It points man to his one and only hope of becoming righteous in the sight of a holy God.

In this first part of Romans Paul knocks all the props out from under everyone. He knew that men will lean on anything they can except God. But when anyone finishes reading these Scriptures he should be convinced that without God's help he is finished!

FOUR

The Judge Provides the Remedy

FROM ROMANS 1:16 TO 3:20 we see man's ruin. Now we are to see God's righteousness. This is the heart of the epistle.

Sin created a terrible crisis. Now we see the *God* of the crisis. Man was completely unable to help himself. He was guilty and could do nothing to make himself right before the Almighty. Judged by his own works he was condemned. The Law could not help him.

The problem was beyond solution by man, but it became God's concern. He found a way. Without sacrificing His own righteousness God made a way to bestow His righteousness upon sinful man.

Thus we have God-provided righteousness. Man can be justified through Jesus Christ. To be righteous means to be right. This is the only way anyone can go to heaven. They must be right.

Can you imagine a judge in an earthly courtroom declaring to the accused, "I find you guilty; you are sentenced to death," and then saying, "But I have found a way to set you free while still carrying out complete justice." If such a thing has ever happened we haven't heard of it. But this is exactly the message of the gospel. It's what we mean by the term "justification." In fact, "righteousness" and "justification" come from the same root word.

How can God be just and still pardon the guilty? This is a problem that man could not solve. When the law is broken the offender must be punished. If he is set free there might as well be no law. From then on everyone would scorn the law and break it freely. Justice would disappear.

But God's wisdom is far beyond man's. God did punish sin, but He punished it in the person of His own innocent Son on the Cross. The sentence was carried out when Jesus hung on Calvary. He suffered the same tortures in His spirit that a lost soul will suffer in hell. He was actually forsaken by God—just as anyone in hell is forsaken by Him. When a sinner repents and accepts Christ's sacrifice for himself his guilt is transferred to the Lord Jesus. Since the sin has already been punished in the very body of God's Son on the Cross it cannot be punished again. The sinner goes free. His debt to God has been paid. He could not do it himself, but the Lord Jesus could, and did.

"But Now."

"But now the righteousness of God without the law is manifested, being witnessed by the law and the prophets; even the righteousness of God which is by faith of Jesus Christ unto all and upon all them that believe; for there is no difference: for all have sinned, and come short of the glory of God" (Romans 3:21-23).

What a relief to hear those two words, "But now." The Judge does not execute the sentence He has pronounced. He steps down, and in the person of His Son takes the place of the condemned one.

"But now"—these words announce a new era. They

34

are words of joy. The Law was of no avail, but now we shall see what God does.

Paul brings into sharp focus the past and the present. He speaks of the Law that was, and the gospel that is. Grace, love, and faith in Christ are in the spotlight, distinct from Law and works.

The Scriptures make it clear that man cannot make the smallest claim to God's favor. Personal worthiness is completely out of the picture. Grace is God's *unmerited* favor. It is unearned. That is the basis of man's salvation.

If a man could be saved by his own righteousness, then Christ's righteousness would be worthless. Man could boast when he reaches heaven. The Bible teaches that no man living can be justified by what he is or does. He is condemned for what he is and for what he does. He is justified by what *Christ* has done *for* him.

"The righteousness of God without the Law"—this is a truth that shines like a beacon light throughout Romans. The Law was like a giant finger of accusation constantly pointed at the sinner. Every day it reminded him, "You're all wrong and you can't get right." The more he struggled the worse his dilemma became. He knew the Law said, "Thou shalt not," but he found himself doing those forbidden things anyway. He could not control his sinful nature. *It* controlled *him*.

The Law was like a ladder reaching to heaven, challenging man to climb up on it to everlasting life. But every time he made it up a few rungs he fell all the way back. Each day he picked himself up and gave it another try. But the results were always the same. The sinful nature dominated. Man was sin's slave.

"But now." A new day has dawned. Jesus has come. God so loved the world that He gave His only be-gotten Son. The way has been opened. God wants man so much that He gave the best He had to rescue him.

"Unto All."

Look at that 22nd verse again: "Even the righ-teousness of God which is by faith of Jesus Christ unto all and upon all them that believe." Here the spotlight is on the scope of righteousness. It is "unto all and upon all them that believe, for there is no difference." God makes no distinction because of na-tionality, social status, or anything else. There is no difference among men in regard to sin. *All* have sinned. All have come short of the glory of God. And God's salvation is to all.

There is no difference in the fact of sin. There may be degrees of sin, but evil is evil regardless of the amount or intensity. Poison is poison, whether it is a drop or a gallon. Sinners shall be judged, and it will be according to their works.

Neither is there any difference in the fact of God's love for us. God does not love anyone for what he is, but because of what *He* is. Sin does not affect God's love for us. It does, however, make us incapable of receiving those blessings offered by that love. If we draw the shades we do not stop the sun from shining. We simply shut ourselves off from the light.

Some sinners live a respectable moral life. Others go to the depths of degradation. But one sinner needs God's remedy as much as the other. There is no dif-ference in their guilt. The thief, the prostitute, and the murderer are sinners. So is the man who does not do these things but has never accepted Christ. God's sentence of death is not upon the outcasts and criminals of society alone. It is upon all. There is no difference.

All have "come short," Paul declares. Man's difficulty lies in comparing himself with other men. It is not hard to find someone who is worse than we are. But no man is the yardstick by which God measures other men. God measures everyone by the same rule. And everyone comes short. Man is like a foot ruler trying to be as long as a yardstick. No matter how hard he struggles he cannot come up to God's standard. Only Jesus did that. Man's only hope is to accept Jesus.

Everyone of us is included in God's "all." When God looks down on the world He does not see a mass of humanity. He sees individual souls. He sees lives that need personal redemption. That is why He sent His Son to be a personal Saviour. God deals with each of us as though there were no other.

BY HIS GRACE

"Being justified freely by his grace through the redemption that is in Christ Jesus" (Romans 3:24).

The word *justify* is a legal term. It means "to declare righteous." As reflected in the New Testament it means even more than to forgive sin and remove condemnation. It means also to place the offender in the position of righteousness.

A criminal can be pardoned by the governor, but he cannot be reinstated in society as one who has never broken the law. But God's plan provides for this kind of miracle. He blots out the past with all its sin, and then considers the sinner as though he had never sinned. The guilty one is pronounced "justified." Wonderful? That's not the word for it!

The bestowal of righteousness is "freely by his

grace." Man had nothing with which to justify himself. He could not measure up to God's demands. God could not come down to what man could offer. The gap between them was too wide to be bridged by any human means.

But God pardoned and justified man through grace, without any price being paid by man. Salvation through grace eliminates two dangers: first, the self-righteousness of self-effort; second, the feeling that one can never be saved at all.

The basis for the bestowal of God's grace is "through the redemption that is in Christ Jesus." How can God call a sinner righteous when he has done nothing to earn it? The answer is that Jesus earned it for the sinner. Christ is our representative, and He is righteous. By trusting in Him we share His righteousness. Because God accepts Him, He accepts us. We appear before God as clothed in the righteousness of Christ.

"Grace" is the keynote of the gospel. "Works" was the keynote of the Law. The sound of the Law is a sharp blast of condemnation. The sound of the gospel is a beautiful melody of redemption.

The word *grace* even appears in secular usage. You may have a payment due on a certain date. But your creditor gives you a "grace period." He could rightfully demand the whole payment when it is due and take action against you if you are late. But for no reason except his own kindness he allows you extra time. It is not something you can demand. You have no right to it. It is an unmerited favor. Any human illustration is puny when we are trying to describe God's work, but perhaps some of them can help us see the picture a little more clearly.

"Whom God hath set forth to be a propitiation through faith in his blood, to declare his righteousness for the remission of sins that are past, through the forbearance of God; to declare, I say, at this time His righteousness: that he might be just, and the justifier of him which believeth in Jesus" (Romans 3:25,26).

Justification is purchased through the sacrifice of Christ. "Propitiation" means bringing together. In this case it means the bringing together of God and man. Access to God is a great privilege. It has been purchased at a great price—the blood of Christ.

Paul does not point to Christ's good example or teaching, but to His blood, as he deals with these great truths. Our Lord was indeed a perfect example. His teaching is the rule by which the Christian lives. But it was His death that saved us. If He had not shed His blood there would have been no salvation for anyone.

By His death Jesus appeased the righteous wrath of God. Sin kept God and man apart. Christ dealt with sin so that this separation can be ended.

The effect of Christ's redemption was retroactive (Romans 3:25). It seemed that God overlooked sin in past ages. Men sinned and sinned, yet seemed not to reap the wages of sin. Did God ignore sin? On occasions He inflicted punishment, but not the full penalty. If God had punished sin fully the whole human race would have been destroyed. God sent Christ to die to demonstrate His justice in view of the tolerance He had seemingly shown. Thus Christ's death reached back to the sins of the past as well as forward to the sins yet to be committed.

Christ took our place. It was the place of the

cursed (Galatians 3:13). He was made sin (2 Corinthians 5:21). God treated His Son on the Cross as though He were a sinner guilty of breaking all of His laws. When Jesus rose from the dead it was proof that God had accepted the sacrifice He made.

Saved men have always praised the blood of Jesus. They have written great hymns about it. They testify of it. When at last we are safe in heaven we shall continue to sing of the precious Blood (Revelation 5: 9). That Blood has blotted out our bad record. It has erased our guilt.

The Key Is Faith

"Where is boasting then? It is excluded. By what law? of works? Nay, but by the law of faith. Therefore we conclude that a man is justified by faith without the deeds of the law" (Romans 3:27,28).

To have faith means to depend on another. When you make a trip by plane you have faith in the pilot and crew. You are completely dependent on them to get you to your destination. We are cleansed by Christ's blood when we have faith in it. When we become completely dependent on His atonement we are born again into the family of God.

John G. Patton was a missionary to the South Sea Islands about 100 years ago. When he was translating the New Testament into the native tongue he had great difficulty finding words for "faith" and "believe." One day a native teacher came in hot and tired from a long walk. He set himself on a chair, put his feet on another, using a native word meaning, "I am resting my whole weight here." Immediately Patton knew he had the difficulty of translation solved. The natives came to know that "faith" and "believe" mean to rest the weight of mind and heart on Christ.

When you come home and find your door locked

the first thing you reach for is your key. If you did not have it there would be a problem. But it is all solved quickly when that key is put in the lock. God's door of salvation swings open so easily when we use the key of faith.

ONE GOD FOR EVERYONE

"Is he the God of the Jews only? is he not also of the Gentiles? Yes, of the Gentiles also: seeing it is one God, which shall justify the circumcision by faith, and uncircumcision through faith. Do we then make void the law through faith? God forbid. Yea, we establish the law" (Romans 3:29-31).

There can be no boasting if man examines his record. It is black. God does not deal one way with the Jew and another way with the Gentile. The Jew does not have one God and the Gentile a different one. God is impartial in His justice, and impartial in His pardon.

Man is justified by faith. It is the same for Jew and Gentile. No one has any advantage over another.

The law of faith does no violence to the law of Moses. The believer, through Christ, finds new sacredness to the law's commands. He receives a new power to fulfill them.

FIVE

Here's Your Proof

NEW IDEAS AREN'T EASILY ACCEPTED. To the people of Paul's day his teaching about justification seemed revolutionary. They thought it was a new doctrine. Their thinking was saturated with the Law.

Paul first has to show these folks that man has no righteousness of his own. They must realize that no one can justify himself. The whole human race is included—Jew and Gentile alike. All of them stand condemned without exception.

Now Paul is going back to the Old Testament to show that justification by faith is not a new doctrine at all. It was recognized centuries before by two of Israel's great men, Abraham and David.

Through the first three chapters of Romans Paul is dealing with principles. Now he turns to personalities. He has been standing in the classroom, explaining. Now he moves to the laboratory to demonstrate.

No two men ranked higher in Jewish esteem than Abraham and David. The Jews boasted of "Abraham, our father." They expected the Messiah from the line of David. When Jews wished to revel in their spiritual superiority they referred to these leaders.

Paul proceeds to show that neither Abraham nor

David rested in his own righteousness. Rather, they trusted in the mercy of God. God declared both righteous, but it was in the same way that we are justified. Abraham lived before the Law was given, and David lived under the Law. Both men were justified by faith, not works.

In Romans 3:21 Paul has already declared that "righteousness . . . without the law is manifested, being witnessed by the law and the prophets." The prop he must knock out from under the Jews was their reliance on the Law. As long as they leaned on that, they could not accept justification by faith. Human pride delights in thinking good works can please God. The apostle declares over and over that any attempt to earn salvation only leads to condemnation. Man's idea of righteousness and God's standard of righteousness are worlds apart. Paul skillfully shows that justification by faith is not a brand-new doctrine. It has always been God's way for those with enough spiritual perception to recognize it.

FIRST WITNESS—ABRAHAM

"What shall we say then that Abraham our father, as pertaining to the flesh, hath found? For if Abraham were justified by works, he hath whereof to glory, but not before God. For what saith the Scripture? Abraham believed God, and it was counted unto him for righteousness. Now to him that worketh is the reward not reckoned of grace, but of debt. But to him that worketh not, but believeth on him that justifieth the ungodly, his faith is counted for righteousness" (Romans 4:1-5).

Romans is a law book. Its terms are law terms. The indictment against sin and sinners has been argued, and every plea known to legal practice has been exhausted. We have come to the great truth of

43

justification. At Calvary "mercy and truth are met together; righteousness and peace have kissed each other" (Psalm 85:10).

But the Jews could not understand that righteousness could come apart from the Law. To them it seemed unscriptural. Notice how Paul builds support for the doctrine. He goes to the Old Testament and proves that justification by faith is scriptural.

If any man is held up as an example of righteousness it is Abraham. He was called "the Friend of God" (James 2:23). He was a justified man, but his righteousness was not based on works. The only reason he is declared righteous is that he believed God. Abraham was a sinner, but he put his faith in the Redeemer who was to come. Jesus told a group of Jews, "Your father Abraham rejoiced to see my day: and he saw it, and was glad" (John 8:56).

Abraham believed that the promised Saviour was to be born from a descendant of his. He received righteousness on the basis of trusting that One who was to come (Galatians 3:13-16).

When we earn something by works it is wages. If it is received without work it is a gift. This is the great contrast between the Law and grace. The Law was all works. Grace is a gift which man cannot possibly earn. It is received by faith.

Lawyers bring their strongest witnesses when they argue their cases. To the Jews there could be no more powerful witness than Abraham. If they could understand that Abraham believed what Paul was teaching it would have great weight. Lifelong beliefs and prejudices do not die easily. Paul is not content merely to argue. He must base his plea on the Word of God. The Old Testament was the Bible of the Jews. The apostle uses it to prove the truth.

44

"Even as David also describeth the blessedness of the man, unto whom God imputeth righteousness without works, saying, Blessed are they whose iniquities are forgiven, and whose sins are covered. Blessed is the man to whom the Lord will not impute sin" (Romans 4:6-8).

No one could appreciate forgiveness and mercy more than David. He was a man after God's own heart, yet he committed the double crime of adultery and murder. Certainly anyone with this record could not claim justification by works!

In the case of Abraham Paul deals with the positive side of justification. David's experience touches the negative side. It shows that God does not impute sin to those He justifies. How thankful sinful man should be that this is true.

Paul is quoting from the 32nd Psalm. This was apparently written after David went through his terrible experience of sinning, trying to ignore the sin, and finally repenting. How graphically he describes his torture:

"When I kept silence, my bones waxed old through my roaring all the day long. For day and night thy hand was heavy upon me: my moisture is turned into the drought of summer. I acknowledged my sin unto thee, and mine iniquity have I not hid. I said, I will confess my transgressions unto the Lord; and thou forgavest the iniquity of my sin" (Psalm 32:3-5).

David's experience was no different from that of many sinners. His description of his inner agony is what we call "conviction." There is misery and despair as the sinner tries to ignore his guilt. His mind, his nerves, his emotions, and even his body are affected. He cannot sleep. The Holy Spirit is pointing His finger at his black record. He knows it is true, but doesn't want to admit it.

Some try to ease their conscience by doing something they consider good. This may bring temporary relief, but it will not last. There is still the nagging realization that all is not well between the soul and God.

David finally did what every sinner should do. He prayed, and he confessed. Immediately there came the assurance of forgiveness. But it was not the result of anything good he had done. It was all through God's mercy, which he received by faith. Jesus' death on the Cross has made it possible for *all* sinners to be pardoned. Once God pardons, He does not charge the sin to one's account.

CEREMONIES DON'T SAVE

"Cometh this blessedness then upon the circumcision only, or upon the uncircumcision also? for we say that faith was reckoned to Abraham for righteousness. How was it then reckoned? when he was in circumcision, or in uncircumcision? Not in circumcision, but in uncircumcision. And he received the sign of circumcision, a seal of the righteousness of the faith which he had yet being uncircumcised: that he might be the father of all them that believe, though they be not circumcised; that righteousness might be imputed unto them also: and the father of circumcision to them who are not of the circumcision only, but who also walk in the steps of that faith of our father Abraham, which he had being yet uncircumcised" (Romans 4:9-12).

The Jews believed circumcision was part of the

46

reason for Abraham's justification. Paul points out that his justification took place *before* he was circumcised. In fact, it was at least 14 years before.

This portion of the Scripture emphasizes that the sacraments and ceremonies of the church do not save. There are some today who believe that salvation is through sacraments. This is emphatically unscriptural.

Just as circumcision did not bring righteousness to Old Testament Jews, so baptism does not bring regeneration. Human works have been rejected as a basis for righteousness. So must religious ordinances and ceremonies be rejected as a means of salvation. Neither baptism nor the Lord's Supper has power to save. Redemption is through the blood of Jesus Christ alone. To add anything else is to bring dishonor to the Blood atonement of our Lord.

Under the New Testament outward circumcision is no longer a ceremony. The work of the gospel is inward, not outward. Salvation does its work in a man's spirit, not his flesh.

Once a person has been saved, church ordinances are meaningful. They bring a blessing. One who has found Christ *should* be baptized in water. He should take Communion. These are matters of obedience on the part of a Christian. The main point to remember is that they do not save. When an unsaved person engages in these ordinances they are meaningless and empty. They do not make a man righteous any more than circumcision made the Old Testament Jews righteous.

Ceremonies are often pleasing to the flesh, but they cannot touch the inward man.

"OF FAITH . . . BY GRACE"

"For the promise, that he should be the heir of

47

the world, was not to Abraham, or to his seed, through the law, but through the righteousness of faith. For if they which are of the law be heirs, faith is made void, and the promise made of none effect: because the law worketh wrath: for where no law is, there is no transgression. Therefore it is of faith, that it might be by grace, to the end the promise might be sure to all the seed; not to that only which is of the law, but to that also which is of the faith of Abraham; who is the father of us all, (as it is written, I have made thee a father of many nations)" (Romans 4:13-17).

God's promise to Abraham was given prior to the Law. It was a promise based on grace. There is no other way to receive anything from the Lord.

Christ the Redeemer was the object of God's promise to Abraham. The Law was instituted only until the Saviour came. It was "our schoolmaster to bring us unto Christ" (Galatians 3:24). But when Christ came, the schoolmaster's work was done. "The promise . . . was not . . . through the law, but through the righteousness of faith" (Romans 4:13).

The Old Covenant and the New Covenant cannot be mixed together. When works are made the center of everything, grace is pushed out. Abraham was given a promise that could not be fulfilled in the natural. But he believed God!

Some have used the expression, "By grace, through faith, plus nothing." This well defines the principle of the gospel. It is exactly what Paul says in Ephesians 2:8,9: "For by grace are ye saved through faith, and that not of yourselves: it is the gift of God: not of works, lest any man should boast."

Justification by faith does not appeal to man's egotism. It eliminates any possibility of boasting of his part in his own salvation. To think of salvation by works is very appealing to the carnal mind. Man feels good if he can do something he thinks is righteous.

But man's ways are not God's ways. When we are saved it is because of what God has done through Christ. Our only part is to believe and to accept Christ as our personal Saviour. We are pardoned because a God of grace chooses to pardon us. The plan of salvation is His; not ours. We dare not substitute any schemes of our own. Any satisfaction they might bring us is very temporary.

The Man Who Didn't Stagger

"Before him whom he believed, even God, who quickeneth the dead and calleth those things which be not as though they were: who against hope believed in hope, that he might become the father of many nations, according to that which was spoken, So shall thy seed be. And being not weak in faith, he considered not his own body now dead, when he was about a hundred years old, neither yet the deadness of Sarah's womb: he staggered not at the promise of God through unbelief; but was strong in faith, giving glory to God; and being fully persuaded, that, what he had promised, he was able also to perform. And therefore it was imputed to him for righteousness" (Romans 4:17-22).

In this passage we see that faith brings an individual into right relationship with the Lord.

God promised that Abraham should be "a father of many nations." This was beyond natural possibility. Abraham and his wife were both too old to expect children. But in spite of the natural obstacles, Abraham did not stagger. His faith was not wobbly. It

49

was strong and steadfast. He believed what was promised because it was God who *made* the promise.

Abraham's faith was in God. Faith is more than a doctrine. It is a heartfelt trust in a Person. It is confidence in God's character and God's Word. Saving faith is trust in what Christ has done on the Cross. It is an unshakable belief in all of the benefits resulting from His blood atonement.

Because Abraham believed in this Person, he could reckon "those things which be not as though they were." He was not trusting some human idea. His confidence was in the Word of the Living God. Without faith it is impossible to have communion with the Lord. It is impossible to have contact with Him. When faith is absent, God's works cannot be comprehended nor understood.

The things of God are spiritual and invisible. The natural eye cannot see them and the natural mind cannot understand them. Faith is the eye that sees. Without that eye man is blind and cannot have fellowship with an unseen God.

Faith is the hand by which man grasps eternal things. Without that hand, no such grasp is possible.

When God speaks, nothing is impossible. Natural obstacles do not count when He is involved. The unconverted mind staggers at divine promises, but the mind that is spiritually illuminated does not. Staggering faith will soon be *fallen* faith.

"IF WE BELIEVE"

"Now it was not written for his sake alone, that it was imputed to him; but for us also, to whom it shall be imputed, if we believe on him that raised up Jesus our Lord from the dead; who was delivered for our offenses, and was raised again for our justification" (Romans 4:23-25).

We must act on the promises of God with the same assurance Abraham showed. Satan will make a sinner believe it is impossible for him to be forgiven. He will lead him to believe that he has gone too far to be pardoned. Naturally speaking, this would be true, but we are not dealing with the natural. We are dealing with God.

The story of Abraham's faith and justification is not merely ancient history. It is written for the benefit of believers in all ages. Abraham looked ahead and believed what God was going to do through Jesus' death and resurrection. We look *back* and see what Christ has already done. God asks of us the same simple faith He found in Abraham.

SIX

Here's Real Living

PAUL HAS BEEN TELLING US the "how" of justification. Now he starts dealing with experience. He wants us to know how justification affects an individual in his everyday life.

We are not involved with theories. Salvation really works! Justification is the beginning of a brand-new life.

Paul uses contrasts. He talks about what we inherited through Adam; then tells us what we inherited through Christ. What we got through Adam was sin and death. But in Christ it is righteousness and life.

Jesus is sometimes called the second, or last, Adam, because He—like the first Adam—is the Head of a new creation. His is a spiritual one. Through the first Adam we were made bad. In the second Adam we can be made good.

Righteousness that comes by faith gives us assurance of future glory. The best is yet to come. The path of the justified gets brighter every day.

ACCESS BY FAITH

"Therefore being justified by faith, we have peace with God through our Lord Jesus Christ: by whom also we have access by faith into this grace wherein we stand, and rejoice in hope of the glory of God. And not only so, but we glory in tribulations also; knowing that tribulation worketh patience; and patience, experience; and experience, hope: and hope maketh not ashamed; because the love of God is shed abroad in our hearts by the Holy Ghost which is given unto us" (Romans 5:1-5).

In Chapter 3 Christ is set forth as the One who made atonement for our sins. In Chapter 4 we see Him raised from the dead for our justification. Chapter 5 describes the standing we have with God now that we have been justified through Christ.

"Therefore being justified by faith, we have. . . ." You could start right there with a long list of things we have as Christians. They are endless. The blessing mentioned in this verse is "peace with God." This is no small thing. Millions would give all they have for peace. They seek it every place else but in God.

You might know of a place where treasure is stored and is available to anyone wishing to claim it. But this would do you no good if there were no way to enter the place. Without access there would be no means of claiming the riches.

Access to God is denied the sinner. Every time he tries to make contact with the Lord he finds the door blocked. Justification changes this dilemma. A door is opened. God says, "Come in!"

Peace with God, and access to Him, are based on Christ's work at Calvary. These blessings are not obtained by striving or working. They are received through faith in what Christ has already accomplished. His work of atonement is the only work God can accept.

53

Access to God is really the first benefit of justification. Note also the phrase, "wherein we stand." The believer has been brought into a place in Christ that is one of standing, not falling. Men sometimes talk of the "standing" of someone in the community, in the church, on the job, etc. Paul is speaking of something far more important—our standing with the Lord. Once it was all bad. We had *no* standing except that of being lost. But now we stand before Him in a state of grace. We have been justified. We are His children. The door into His presence is always open.

He Loved Us When We Were Bad

"For when we were yet without strength, in due time Christ died for the ungodly. For scarcely for a righteous man will one die: yet peradventure for a good man some would even dare to die. But God commendeth His love toward us, in that, while we were yet sinners, Christ died for us" (Romans 5:6-8).

What Paul says here is easily understood. It would not be unusual to find someone willing to die for a good man. But to die for someone who is not only wicked but who actually hates you is a different story. Yet this is exactly what Jesus did. He died for us when we were at our worst. There is no sinner so low that God's love does not reach him.

Was it not significant that the first person to benefit from Christ's atoning death was a thief? He was part of the dregs of society; yet Christ saved him in his last hours on earth. We don't have to be criminals to need God's mercy. We have sinned just as much as that thief on the cross, and we are *just as lost.*

Christ came "in due time." At the right moment God sent His Son to the world. His plan of salvation was designed before He even created the human race.

The plan was ready before a sin was even committed. Salvation is not a hastily conceived idea. It was not a quick reaction to an emergency.

Naturally man was given the opportunity to obey God. But the Lord knew ahead of time man would fail. So He provided for that failure before it ever took place.

God commendeth His love "toward" us. It is pointed in our direction. We are the ones who need it. When a man is in danger of drowning, the life preserver will be thrown to the spot where he is. When man was in danger of perishing eternally God sent the lifeline of His love right to him. Jesus came all the way from heaven to earth to bring deliverance to those who need it.

God does not divide the world into various kinds of sinners—very bad, medium bad, and fairly good. We are simply sinners. That makes us lost. We would have perished forever if God had not intervened. First there was the miracle of Christ's virgin birth, by which God became man. There was the miracle of His sinless life among sinful men. There was the miracle of His sacrificial death. It was not a martyrdom, but an atonement. And the miracle of His resurrection sealed the transaction forever. He was raised for our justification.

RECONCILIATION

"Much more then, being now justified by his blood, we shall be saved from wrath through him. For if, when we were enemies, we were reconciled to God by the death of his Son; much more, being reconciled, we shall be saved by his life. And not only so, but we also joy in God through our Lord Jesus Christ, by whom we have now received the atonement" (Romans 5:9-11).

"Reconciliation" is a beautiful word. It speaks of those who were once far apart being brought together. God and man were worlds apart because of the barrier of sin. Jesus took each by the hand and brought them together at the Cross.

"All things are of God, who hath reconciled us to himself by Jesus Christ, and hath given to us the ministry of reconciliation; to wit, that God was in Christ, reconciling the world unto himself, not imputing their trespasses unto them; and hath committed unto us the word of reconciliation" (2 Corinthians 5:18,19).

Reconciliation produces fellowship. You cannot have fellowship with someone from whom you are estranged. You might nod and speak in passing, but that's all. There will be no close contact. But when you are reconciled there's a completely different relationship.

Before our justification God was simply a name to us. We may have believed He existed, but our thoughts about Him were vague and uncertain. There was nothing personal involved. In fact, there could not be. We may even have prayed to Him at times, but there was no real communion.

Now, through Christ, a radical change has taken place. We can call God "Father" with no embarrassment or strain. We don't save our prayers for tight places and moments of trouble. Prayer becomes as natural as breathing. We talk to the Lord all day long. He is never far from our thoughts. He becomes the most important part of our life.

We must remember that reconciliation is a work of God. He had to initiate it, for we could not. No matter how much we wanted to be reconciled it was not in our power to bring it about. God wanted to be reconciled to us even more than we wanted it. So He made it possible at a terrible cost to himself. He gave his only begotten Son. It is good that this is not a work of ours. We are so prone to bragging that we would spend eternity telling about it. Instead, our song is always about Him.

DEATH'S REIGN

"Wherefore, as by one man sin entered into the world, and death by sin; and so death passed upon all men, for that all have sinned: for until the law sin was in the world: but sin is not imputed when there is no law. Nevertheless death reigned from Adam to Moses, even over them that had not sinned after the similitude of Adam's transgression, who is the figure of him that was to come" (Romans 5:12-14).

Here Paul uses contrast to show us the benefits of justification. He talks of Adam and Christ to show what we were by nature and what we are by grace.

The great truth of verses 12-21 is that a representative sinned and involved all mankind with him. Adam, the first man, was our representative. When he sinned we all sinned. When he died we all died. His one sin was a representative act. It is the ground upon which all humans were condemned by God. All were made guilty by Adam's one act. "Through the offense of one many be dead."

In Adam our heritage is one of sin, offense, disobedience, judgment, condemnation, and death. Every man who has not been justified by Christ is "in Adam." And "in Adam all die" (1 Corinthians 15:22).

Adam's race inherited an evil tendency: a leaning toward sin. This manifests itself in sinful acts. Man has become sinful through Adam's sin. He is a sinner because of Adam's disobedience. Paul says we were "by nature the children of wrath" (Ephesians 2:3).

Death is the penalty for sin. Every funeral procession reminds us of the effect of Adam's sin. The existence of death cannot be explained apart from the existence of sin. If man had never sinned he would have never died. When one is ruled by sin, death inevitably follows.

The death of the body is not the only death the Bible talks about. There is also spiritual death. A sinner is dead to God. Just as a dead man cannot respond to those around him, a sinner cannot respond to God. There is nothing in him that reacts when God moves or speaks. Sin has killed him spiritually.

There is also that final death on the other side of the grave. The Bible calls it "the second death" (Revelation 20:14). Physical death is not the end of man's existence. He *never* ceases to exist. But if he leaves the world without Christ his very existence is such a terrible thing that it can only be described as a "second death." All the jokes men might tell about hell cannot minimize this awful truth.

THE FREE GIFT

"But not as the offense, so also is the free gift: for if through the offense of one many be dead, much more the grace of God, and the gift by grace, which is by one man, Jesus Christ, hath abounded unto many. And not as it was by one that sinned, so is the gift: for the judgment was by one to condemnation, but the free gift is of many offenses unto justification. For if by one man's offense death reigned by one; much more they which receive abundance of grace and of the gift of righteousness shall reign in life by one, Jesus Christ" (Romans 5:15-17).

In the first Adam all men were made sinners. But sinners are made righteous in the Second Adam. The effect of sin was separation from God—spiritual death. Because of God's holiness sinful man could have no fellowship with Him; only separation from Him.

A great gulf separates sinful man from a holy God. Christ's death was God's way of bridging this gulf. The eternal Son of God became the perfect Son of Man. He was the one Person who could take on himself the guilt, the penalty, and the effects of sin. He was the only One who could make it possible for the sinner to be transformed into a righteous person in God's sight.

Our sins are imputed to Christ. He became sin in our place. He bore the penalty and guilt that were rightfully ours. When we accept Him, His righteousness is imputed to us.

"Who his own self bare our sins in his own body; on the tree, that we, being dead to sins, should live unto righteousness: by whose stripes ye were healed" (1 Peter 2:24).

"The free gift!" What amazing words! This is the theme of the gospel. It is what salvation is all about. What we could not do, God has done. What we could not earn, God has given.

For the Christian, death's reign is over. Even if he dies physically the sting of death is gone. Death is simply the gateway to life for God's children. There will be no "second death" for the believer. Everlasting life is his heritage. And instead of being dead to God he is alive to Him. He responds to Him. He has communion with Him. He is a new creature in Christ.

We were the ones who offended God. But it was God who took steps to end our exile from Him. He is not willing that any should perish. Those who do must break down every barrier He has placed in front of them.

ABOUNDING GRACE

"Therefore, as by the offense of one judgment came upon all men to condemnation; even so by the righteousness of one the free gift came upon all men unto justification of life. For as by one man's disobedience many were made sinners, so by the obedience of one shall many be made righteous. Moreover the law entered, that the offense might abound. But where sin abounded, grace did much more abound: that as sin hath reigned unto death, even so might grace reign through righteousness unto eternal life by Jesus Christ our Lord" (Romans 5:18-21).

A key word in Romans 5:12-21 is "one." In those verses it occurs 12 times. One man brings the curse of sin and death. One man brings eternal life to all who believe.

Without choice, all men are "in Adam." The whole creation was dragged to ruin in him. The last Adam, Christ, brings all men who believe into a supernatural generation. We died with Him; we rose with Him; we sit in heavenly places with Him. Offsetting "sin" and "death" is the bestowment of "grace," "righteousness," and "eternal life." These are ours "by Jesus Christ our Lord."

Before Christ came, sin "abounded." It ran rampant. It overflowed. The whole human race was being swept along by it to destruction. Since Christ has come, grace abounds. It is a mighty river that swallows up the river of sin and bears every believer along to heaven.

As strong as sin is, God's grace is stronger. As powerful as Satan is, Christ is more powerful. As invincible as death seems, eternal life through Christ wipes death out.

There is no part of life that God's grace does not cover. We are saved by grace, and we are kept by it. Grace sustains us daily. God's unmerited favor makes us more than conquerors in the battles of life.

Grace "reigns," Paul declares. It is dominant. The Christian has been lifted up above the forces that formerly ruled him. Note the ascending road we are traveling: "Through righteousness, unto eternal life."

God's grace is not a trickle. It is an ocean. It covers our sins. It covers our past and future. It will cover us through all eternity. It has come to us through the precious blood of Christ.

SEVEN

A Slave No Longer

"WHAT SHALL WE SAY THEN? Shall we continue in sin, that grace may abound? God forbid. How shall we, that are dead to sin, live any longer therein? Know ye not, that so many of us as were baptized into Jesus Christ were baptized into his death? Therefore we are buried with him by baptism unto death: that like as Christ was raised up from the dead by the glory of the Father, even so we also should walk in newness of life" (Romans 6:1-4).

It is one thing to become a Christian. It is another thing to live the Christian life. Many new converts, after experiencing the joy of forgiveness, find to their dismay that sin has not been totally conquered in their lives.

This need not be. To some people complete victory over sin appears impossible. But such thinking is an error. We must understand what Christ did for us at Calvary. Just as our salvation depends on Him, so does our victory over sin.

The believer does not sin as long as he abides in Christ. We can sin only by leaving that safe shelter. Jesus declared that no man could pluck us out of the Father's hand. We must conclude, then, that if a believer goes back into sin he does it deliberately.

The subject Paul deals with in these passages is what is often called "sanctification." Up to this point the contrast has been between wrath and justification. Now it is between sin and holiness. Christ gets us out from under the penalty of sin. We must also realize that He delivers us from its power and control. We do not have to "sin a little every day," as some have erroneously suggested.

"Newness of life." This is what salvation is all about. Our old nature is not merely patched up. We have a *new* nature. We are not simply reformed. We are new creatures in Christ Jesus. A Christian is not one who has suddenly decided to be "religious." He is more than a church-joiner. He is one who has experienced victory over the devil's power to keep him bound by sinful habits and practices. Through Christ he has the power to say no to evil things to which he could formerly answer only yes.

THE OLD MAN IS DEAD

"For if we have been planted together in the likeness of his death, we shall be also in the likeness of his resurrection: knowing this that our old man is crucified with him, that the body of sin might be destroyed, that henceforth we should not serve sin. For he that is dead is freed from sin. Now if we be dead with Christ, we believe that we shall also live with him: knowing that Christ being raised from the dead dieth no more; death hath no more dominion over him. For in that he died, he died unto sin once: but in that he liveth, he liveth unto God" (Romans 6:5-10).

"The old man" is an expression of Paul's. It means the old *sinful* man; the person the Christian *used* to be. No matter how much we tried to dress up the old man he was still an ugly creature. We may have even attempted to make him religious. But he was still "the old man," and his master was the devil.

What Paul is teaching involves continuous faith. We do not gain victory over the old man by struggling in our own strength. We gain it by continually believing that when we accepted Christ it was as though the old man died on the Cross with Him. If he is dead he can't keep controlling us, can he?

Paul also uses the expression, "the body of sin." Sins are committed by the body. The Christian has the same physical body as before, but it gets its directions from a redeemed mind and nature. It has come under the control of Christ. By constantly yielding ourselves to the Lord Jesus this "body of sin" is rendered powerless. It is not our physical body that is destroyed, but the old sinful nature. This is what sanctification means. It is both instantaneous and progressive.

The end of all this believing, trusting, and yielding is that "we should not serve sin." Make no mistake about it: sin is slavery. It is rank servitude. It is unthinkable that such servitude should continue to exist in a Christian life.

A dead man can't serve anyone. Paul declares that since the old man died with Christ he cannot continue serving sin. This sets the Christian free. He is no longer in bondage to the whims, desires, and lusts of this "old man."

But there is the positive side. Not only has there been death; there has also been resurrection. The old man died, but a new man has risen with Christ. That new man is the new nature received by the believer at salvation. The old is dead; the new is alive. It cannot be emphasized too strongly that all of this requires a daily act of faith.

We Have a Responsibility, Too

"Likewise reckon ye also yourselves to be dead indeed unto sin, but alive unto God through Jesus Christ our Lord. Let not sin therefore reign in your mortal body, that ye should obey it in the lusts thereof" (Romans 6:11,12).

There are two sides to salvation and the Christian life—the divine side and the human side. God takes care of His responsibility. We must realize that we have our part to play, too.

We could not save ourselves, but we had to make the decision to accept Christ. We cannot win the victory over sin ourselves, but we must resist sin every moment. We cannot sit down passively and say, "All right, Lord, don't let me sin." When temptations come we must turn away from them. When Satan speaks, we must turn a deaf ear. If he pushes us, we must push back. We must rebuke him with the Word just as Jesus did when He was tempted.

We are to "reckon" two things: (1) That the old man has died and the sinful nature rendered powerless; (2) that we are "alive unto God"—new life has been imparted to us.

"Reckon" is a mathematical term. It means "to count; compute; take into account." The Christian is to take into account the fact that he is dead to sin, that he is set free from the old evil nature, that he has been brought into new life, and that, being a new creation, he can live above the desire to sin. The man who was once a sinner but is now saved is under new management!

In Galatians 2:20 Paul wrote, "I am crucified with Christ." The new Paul stood looking at himself nailed to the Cross in the Person of the Lord Jesus. He points to the Cross and says, "There is Paul with his sin and transgression. He is dead."

Of course Paul did not mean he was literally dead. For in the same verse he says, "Nevertheless, I live." What does he mean? He means he was dead to sin, and alive to God. Death severed the union Paul once had with the devil. Thus it broke sin's dominion over him.

Of course, sin is still present in the world. It will not be removed until our salvation becomes complete on the Resurrection Day. But while sin is still present it is rendered powerless except by a deliberate act of reuniting one's self with the enemy.

Paul further stated, "Yet not I, but Christ liveth in me." That's where the victory lies!

THE RIGHT KIND OF YIELDING

"Neither yield ye your members as instruments of unrighteousness unto sin: but yield yourselves unto God, as those that are alive from the dead, and your members as instruments of righteousness unto God. For sin shall not have dominion over you: for ye are not under the law, but under grace" (Romans 6:13, 14).

To yield is to give up; to surrender to a superior force. This is exactly what the sinner does continually. He may think he is his own boss, but nothing could be farther from the truth. Satan is that superior force to which the unsaved individual continually surrenders.

This yielding to Satan makes the sinner an "instrument." Tragically it is the wrong kind of instrument. It is one the devil uses to accomplish his purposes.

When salvation comes, this yielding to Satan stops. Another Force becomes the one to which the Christian yields. That force, of course, is God. Gladly and joy-fully the believer continually surrenders to His will and power. He is still an instrument, but a different kind. He is now used of God for righteous purposes. He becomes a blessing. The Lord uses him to win others to himself.

Under the Law, sin had dominion over men. They tried by their Law-keeping to prove that they could be righteous. But all they proved was that they could not be. Every day they were reminded of their sin-fulness as they brought offerings to the tabernacle and temple. Each sacrificial animal said, "You're a sinner. That's why you have to make this offering."

But Christians are not under the Law. They are under grace. No longer are we reminded that we are sinners. We are reminded that we have been made righteous through Christ. We do not have to strive and fail continually. We yield ourselves to Christ, and His righteousness works through us.

Note the negative and positive in Paul's double challenge: "Neither yield . . . but yield." This involves the making of right choices. We must choose daily between right and wrong. We reckon ourselves to be alive by saying "Yes" to God's will. Someone has said that our will is the steering wheel of our life. The way it is used steers us either onto the right path or the wrong one.

Man is so created that he must be mastered. If we are not mastered by Christ we shall be mastered by Satan. The choice is ours. "Neither yield . . . but yield."

SAVED TO SERVE

"What then? Shall we sin because we are not under law but under grace? May it never be! Do you not know that when you present yourselves to someone as slaves for obedience, you are slaves of the one whom you obey, either of sin resulting in death, or of obedience resulting in righteousness? But thanks be to God that though you were slaves of sin, you became obedient from the heart to that form of teaching to which you were committed, and having been freed from sin, you became slaves of righteousness. I am speaking in human terms because of the weakness of your flesh. For just as you presented your members as slaves to impurity and to lawlessness, resulting in further lawlessness, so now present your members as slaves to righteousness, resulting in sanctification. For when you were slaves of sin, you were free in regard to righteousness" (Romans 6:15-20, *New American Standard Bible*).

You will note that where the King James Version says "servants" the New American Standard Version says "slaves." This is a more accurate rendering, and actually makes the point stronger. Slaves were common in Paul's day. A slave was not his own. He was the property of a master. His days were filled with serving.

When we were in sin we were slaves. Paul says, "Don't think you can stop being a slave because you're saved. The difference is that you are now *God's* slave."

Let no one imagine that salvation is a free ride to heaven. We are saved to serve! This is why we are set free from sin.

The worldly person lives a self-centered life. From that center he sets the pattern of his whole life. The consecrated, or sanctified, person lives a *God*-centered life. All of his activities are designed in accordance with God's will. This is life as it should be. It is the only satisfying life. Someone has said that life is like a wheel. Keep God at the hub and every spoke will be connected to Him.

In this passage Paul again uses contrasts. He speaks of what we were, and what we are. The difference is like day and night. The life of service to sin and the life of service to God are worlds apart—like darkness and light.

Sometimes people are puzzled at the depraved living they see around them. It is not surprising at all. When one serves Satan there is no limit to how far he may go. He is like a car that has lost its brakes. He cannot steer his own life. A fierce personality sits at the wheel, carrying him to destruction. Every Christian should thank God daily that this is no longer true of him.

WAGES AND GIFT

"And what was the result? Evidently not good, since you are ashamed now even to think about those things you used to do, for all of them end in eternal doom. But now you are free from the power of sin and are slaves of God, and his benefits to you include holiness and everlasting life. For the wages of sin is death, but the free gift of God is eternal life through Jesus Christ our Lord" (Romans 6:21-23, *Living Bible Paraphrased*).

Paul calls attention to the sinful fruit of a life ruled by Satan. The test of a tree is its fruit, isn't it? Once a person is saved he realizes how ugly the fruit of sin is. He is ashamed of it; doesn't want to think about it.

God saves us *from* sin; not *in* sin. The fruit of justification is a holy life (sanctification). The final

69

fruit will be glorification. This, of course, will be realized when we reach heaven.

Wages are paid for service rendered. The sinner will get what he earns—death. This means *eternal* death. It means hell; everlasting torment.

What the believer will receive he did not earn. It is a gift—eternal life. Christ earned it *for* him. To Him will be the glory through the ages of eternity.

The Christian has a new destiny. Formerly it was eternal loss. Now it is everlasting reward. The direction of his life has been changed. It is pointed in a direction absolutely opposite to what it was before.

Who would want to go back to those things of which he is now ashamed? The end of those things is death. No matter how much "fun" the sinner thinks he is having, there is a terrible day of reckoning ahead. Payday is coming. A workman in a factory might refuse to collect his wages, but no one can refuse the wages of sin. God will see to it that they are paid in full—with nothing withheld!

Both the wages of sin and the gift of eternal life have their beginning in this present life. The sinner is being paid daily in every area of his life. Eternal life also starts here. Every day the Christian has a taste of what is yet to come!

■ **EIGHT**

The Law Couldn't—Grace Can!

PAUL, AS A JEW, TRIED TO LIVE BY THE LAW until he found Christ. He discovered that, although the Law reveals sin and its results, it is powerless to save.

We are now looking at the subject of sanctification. To be sanctified is to be made holy. The Law could not accomplish this. In the 7th chapter of Romans Paul describes the torture he went through before he discovered the truth.

In Romans 6:14 the apostle declared, "Ye are not under the law, but under grace." This is our standing and privilege as Christians. Paul is anxious to show that the Law has no claim on a believer. The Law demanded death for sin. Christ met this demand when He died on the Cross. He terminated the Law at that time. The believer who died with Him is also dead to the Law. The wages of sin is death, but Christ cancelled those wages. He gives the gift of eternal life to the believer.

Romans 7 describes a man who earnestly desires to be holy by his own efforts. This chapter presents the hopeless conflict between a man's better side and his sinful nature. The lesson is clear: Not only is the Law powerless to save; it cannot sanctify, either. No one can be holy by his own resolutions and endeavors.

Paul uses a rather unusual illustration—that of marriage. It is easily understood, and helps to clarify what he is talking about:

"Don't you understand yet, dear Jewish brothers in Christ, that when a person dies the law no longer holds him in its power? Let me illustrate: when a woman marries, the law binds her to her husband as long as he is alive. But if he dies, she is no longer bound to him; the laws of marriage no longer apply to her. Then she can marry someone else if she wants to. That would be wrong while he was alive, but it is perfectly all right after he dies" (Romans 7:1-3, *Living Bible Paraphrased*).

Death frees an individual from the dominion of the Law. This is illustrated by the marriage vow. The wife is bound to her husband as long as he lives. Both husband and wife are free from each other when either one dies. The one dying is free from the marriage vow, and that death liberates the other, also.

Paul compares the Law to a husband. He teaches that we cannot be married to Christ and enjoy the blessings of grace until the Law is dead to us, or we to the Law.

MARRIED TO ANOTHER

"Your 'husband, your master, used to be the Jewish law; but you 'died,' as it were, with Christ on the cross; and since you are 'dead,' you are no longer 'married to the law,' and it has no more control over you. Then you came back to life again when Christ did, and are a new person. And now you are 'married,' so to speak, to the one who rose from the dead, so that you can produce good fruit, that is, good deeds for God. When your old nature was still active, sinful desires were at work within you, making you want to do whatever God said not to, and producing sinful deeds, the rotting fruit of death. But now you need no longer worry about the Jewish laws and customs because you 'died' while in their captivity, and now you can really serve God; not in the old way, mechanically obeying a set of rules, but in the new way, [with all of your hearts and minds]" (Romans 7:4-6, *Living Bible Paraphrased*).

When the Christian died in Christ to sin, he became dead to the Law. The Law did not die, but we did. We were thus separated from the former "husband" of sin and united with Christ by faith. All of the virtues of Christ's death, in meeting the claims of the Law, became ours. We were set free from the power of sin to which the Law had committed us.

But freedom from the former union is not an end in itself. This severance is for a positive purpose—to be married to another—the One who rose from the dead. By this mystical union with Jesus we have had the payment of the death penalty imputed to us by faith. Death in Christ leads to resurrection in Him. We are united with Him and come under His authority. We share in all of His resources.

The Christian does not struggle to live up to an external standard. He lives to please One who lives within him. He strives to be acceptable to this inward Presence. No longer is life lived on the dreaded principle: "Thou shalt" and "Thou shalt not." The Christian's service to God is based on brand-new principles. No man could obey the Laws given at Mount Sinai. But the believer can keep the commands of the Lord by the empowering presence of the Holy Spirit.

The purpose of this new union with Jesus is that we should produce "good fruit." In our natural condition we "walked according to the course of this world, according to the prince of the power of the air, the spirit that now worketh in the children of disobedience, among whom also we all had our conversation in times past in the lusts of our flesh, fulfilling the desires of the flesh and of the mind; and were by nature the children of wrath, even as others (Ephesians 2:2,3). That kind of living made us ashamed. Now it is different. We live the way God wants us to live because we have the power to do so. This is not because we have suddenly become strong, but because of the presence of Christ within us.

THE GREAT EXPOSER

"Well then, am I suggesting that these laws of God are evil? Of course not! No, the law is not sinful but it was the law that showed me my sin. I would never have known the sin in my heart—the evil desires that are hidden there—if the law had not said, 'You must not have evil desires in your heart.' But sin used this law against evil desires by reminding me that such desires are wrong and arousing all kinds of forbidden desires within me! Only if there were no laws to break would there be no sinning. That is why I felt fine so long as I did not understand what the law really demanded. But when I learned the truth, I realized that I had broken the law and was a sinner, doomed to die" (Romans 7:7-9, *Living Bible Paraphrased*).

Paul does not speak disrespectfully of the Law. It had its place in God's plan. It was a necessary part of man's spiritual education.

The Law was powerless to save and sanctify. This

was not because it wasn't good. It was because of the sinful tendency in human nature known as "the flesh." The difficulty is not with the Law, but with us. The flesh is at fault.

The Law commands and encourages holiness. It exemplifies the holiness of God. The Law is just, for it outlines those things that are just and right.

But Paul discovered that the main thing the Law did for him was to expose his human weakness. The Law made it clear what sin was. It named sins. It defined the path of life which displeased God. As Paul read the commandments, he found himself constantly wanting to do the things the law forbade. He would not have known they were wrong if he had not become aware of the Law.

If a city had no laws there would be no lawbreakers. The Law is what makes a man conscious that his acts are bad. If you are driving too fast, the sign that says, "Speed Limit, 55 miles per hour," reminds you that you are breaking the law. If there were no law you could drive 80 and still feel comfortable in your conscience.

The Law caused men to discover sin. It was like a mirror that constantly showed them how dirty they were inside. Unfortunately it gave no man the power to remove that dirt. So he had to look at his filth without being able to do anything about it. The Law exposed him and then let him suffer his feelings of condemnation.

The reason for all of this is that we might realize our lost condition and turn to Christ for help. The Law made men realize they were sick so they would seek the help of the Great Physician.

THE DEATH PENALTY

"So far as I was concerned, the good law which

was supposed to show me the way of life resulted instead in my being given the death penalty. Sin fooled me by taking the good laws of God and using them to make me guilty of death. But still, you see, the law itself was wholly right and good. But how can that be? Didn't the law cause my doom? How then can it be good? No, it was sin, devilish stuff that it is, that used what was good to bring about my condemnation. So you can see how cunning and deadly and damnable it is. For it uses God's good laws for its own evil purposes" (Romans 7:10-13, *Living Bible Paraphrased*).

The Law not only exposed sin; it demanded a penalty for it. That penalty is death. Physical death is a result of sin, but the death of the body is only the beginning. "It is appointed unto men once to die, but after this the judgment" (Hebrews 9:27).

"The soul that sinneth, it shall die" (Ezekiel 18:20). "Then when lust hath conceived, it bringeth forth sin, and sin, when it is finished, bringeth forth death" (James 5:20). "But the fearful, and unbelieving, and the abominable, and murderers, and whoremongers, and sorcerers, and idolaters, and all liars, shall have their part in the lake which burneth with fire and brimstone, which is the second death" (Revelation 21:8).

"Death" is a word that sobers everyone. But when we talk about death that lasts forever it is too awesome for the human mind to comprehend. Yet this is the penalty decreed for sinners.

Paul is describing thoughts that were in his mind when he was a Jew trying to be righteous by Law-keeping. He thought he was going to be saved by all of his own labors to please God. But what a rude awakening it was when he discovered that the Law had sentenced him to death. No wonder he was such a mighty preacher after he found Christ. The gospel was a message that brought pardon. It saved him from the death penalty.

But the sentence had to be pronounced, or Paul would never have realized his need of a Saviour. As long as he felt he could win favor with God by keeping rules he did not call for help. Only when the Law exposed his sin and sentenced him to death did he seek help outside himself.

As much as it would shock you to hear that you had a deadly disease, you could thank the doctor who diagnosed it because he gave you a chance to be treated and cured. Had there been no Law none of us could have realized our hopeless spiritual plight.

CONFLICT!

"The law is good, then, and the trouble is not there but with me, because I am sold into slavery with Sin as my owner. I don't understand myself at all, for I really want to do what is right, but I can't. I do what I don't want to—what I hate. I know perfectly well that what I am doing is wrong, and my bad conscience proves that I agree with these laws I am breaking. But I can't help myself, because I'm no longer doing it. It is sin inside me that is stronger than I am that makes me do these evil things. I know I am rotten through and through so far as my old sinful nature is concerned. No matter which way I turn I can't make myself do right. I want to, but I can't. When I want to do good, I don't; and when I try not to do wrong, I do it anyway" (Romans 7:14-19, *Living Bible Paraphrased*).

What Paul is describing in these verses is the battle that raged within him when he was trying to be saved by the Law. The very Law he desired so much to obey stirred sinful impulses within him. He was hindered from doing the good he wanted to do, and was driven to doing the things he hated. This civil war rages between the mind and the flesh in all men. This is a graphic picture of a man under the Law who has come to grips with the searching spirituality of the Law, but in his attempt to keep the Law finds himself stymied by indwelling sin.

The key to the meaning of this section is found in the constant repetition of the word "I." There is no mention of the Holy Spirit. Paul only indicated what he was struggling to do in his own strength. When we come to Chapter 8 we find many references to the Holy Spirit. But in this passage there is only the account of what a man goes through trying to please God without the Spirit's help.

You don't have to be a Jew to experience this same inner warfare. Whether you have ever heard of the law of Moses or not, this same struggle has been waged in your own heart, hasn't it? How many good resolutions are made over and over, only to be broken as soon as they are a few minutes old. A man is bound by habits that he sincerely wants to break, but the harder he tries the worse his bondage becomes.

It's a helpless feeling Paul describes. His life had been a battlefield between good and evil, and he was caught in the cross fire. He was like a man trying to climb a hill. He was encouraged when he could take a few steps upward. But there was a terrible letdown when he fell backward farther than he had climbed.

VICTORY!

"Now if I am doing what I don't want to, it is plain where the trouble is: sin still has me in its evil grasp.

It seems to be a fact of life that when I want to do what is right, I inevitably do what is wrong. I love to do God's will so far as my new nature is concerned, but there is something else deep within me, in my lower nature, that is at war with my mind and wins the fight and makes me a slave to the sin that is still within me. In my mind I want to be God's willing servant, but instead I find myself still enslaved to sin. So you see how it is: my new life tells me to do right, but the old nature that is still inside me loves to sin. Oh, what a terrible predicament I'm in! Who will free me from my slavery to this deadly lower nature? Thank God! It has been done by Jesus Christ our Lord. He has set me free" (Romans 7:20-25, *Living Bible Paraphrased*).

The battle with sin is not automatically ended when we are saved. There is the same tendency even with a Christian to struggle for victory in his own power. Even a child of God experiences times when he has wanted to do right and found himself doing wrong. The old nature tries to assert itself, doesn't it?

But Paul ends the discussion on a note of victory. Christ is our sanctification as well as our redemption. We are not saved by human striving, and we are not sanctified by such efforts. Christ freed us from sin and from the Law. As we walk with Him we are also freed from the power that sin would exert over us.

The battles we have are blessings, for they keep us reminded that we must depend on the Lord. Self-confidence is a dangerous thing. If there were no conflicts we might become self-satisfied. We might find it easy not to pray. Even failure can be a benefit as long as we use it as a stepping-stone and do not accept it as permanent.

Jesus won the victory for us at Calvary. He met

the demands of the Law. He paid the only price God could accept for our redemption. If we are abiding in Him we share daily in His victory. There will be testings, but they will end victoriously. Defeat is not God's plan for His children. Victory is!

The 7th chapter of Romans gets us ready for the 8th. Paul paints a black picture of a soul in conflict so the victory that soul wins through Christ will be shown to be all the more glorious.

NINE

The Law of the Spirit of Life

ROMANS 8 IS THE HIGH POINT of the epistle. It begins with "no condemnation," and ends with "no separation." In between there is "no defeat."

The work of the Holy Spirit is introduced. Up to this point the Holy Spirit has been briefly mentioned twice. But there are at least 20 references in this chapter to Him. It is the Spirit who brings deliverance from the dominion of sin.

NO CONDEMNATION

"There is therefore now no condemnation to them which are in Christ Jesus, who walk not after the flesh, but after the Spirit. For the law of the Spirit of life in Christ Jesus hath made me free from the law of sin and death. For what the law could not do, in that it was weak through the flesh, God sending his own Son in the likeness of sinful flesh, and for sin, condemned sin in the flesh: that the righteousness of the law might be fulfilled in us, who walk not after the flesh, but after the Spirit" (Romans 8:1-4).

This universe operates on physical laws instituted by God. There are also spiritual laws that are just as unchanging. The sinner is under the law of sin and death. There is no way for him to escape eternal damnation if he is still under this law at the time of his death. When we are saved we immediately come under a new spiritual law. Paul calls it "the law of the Spirit of life."

Immediately we sense that the condemnation for sin is gone. Our conscience is clear. There is no longer the terrible burden that weighed down our soul. The old law has been superseded. The new law is operating in us!

The law of Moses could not bring this deliverance and victory. It only exhibited the weakness of the flesh. Then God sent His Son to strike the death blow against the law of sin and death. He accomplished this mighty work while He was a man. He was "in the likenss of sinful flesh," but was not a sinner. When He went to the Cross our condemnation was heaped upon Him. When we accept Him as Lord and Saviour that guilt is taken away from us.

"In Christ Jesus" is the key to it all. There is continual condemnation to the unsaved man. But when one is "in Christ Jesus" all that changes.

"AFTER THE FLESH . . . AFTER THE SPIRIT"

"For they that are after the flesh do mind the things of the flesh; but they that are after the Spirit, the things of the Spirit. For to be carnally minded is death, but to be spiritually minded is life and peace. Because the carnal mind is enmity against God: for it is not subject to the law of God, neither indeed can be. So then they that are in the flesh cannot please God. But ye are not in the flesh, but in the Spirit, if so be that the Spirit of God dwell in you. Now if any man have not the Spirit of Christ he is none of his" (Romans 8:5-9).

When we are "after" something, we are inclined in that direction. They that are "after the flesh" have their spirits constantly tuned to what the flesh (human nature) wants. To live such a life is called "carnal" in the Bible. It is displeasing to God because it is self-centered.

To be "after the Spirit" means to be inclined in the direction of the Spirit's leading. They that are after the Spirit are Christ-centered. They seek first the kingdom of God and His righteousness. They are more concerned about spiritual matters than earthly things.

Paul says that to be after the flesh, or carnally minded, leads inevitably to death. First there is that spiritual death that makes one unresponsive to God. In the end there is everlasting death.

To be after the Spirit, or spiritually minded, produces results that are exactly opposite. There is true spiritual life. The heart is responsive to God. There is peace of mind and spirit. And the life that begins at salvation is everlasting.

Our victory through Christ depends on the extent to which we walk after the Spirit. Sad to say, some Christians become carnal! When this happens, victory disappears. There is frustration, defeat, and despair. Complete backslidng may follow. This is not what God intends. His will is that we abide in Christ and walk in the Spirit.

God has never changed His principles of righteousness. But He made provision for changing human nature. He has made available a new spiritual power that is released into human lives through the atoning work of Jesus Christ. This power is for all who reject the ways of the flesh and choose the ways of the Spirit.

When our life is in Christ He imparts new desires

and affections. A holy life is the result. A saved person need not live "after the flesh." The old nature has no place in the life redeemed by Christ.

CHRIST IN YOU

"And if Christ be in you, the body is dead because of sin; but the Spirit is life because of righteousness. But if the Spirit of him that raised up Jesus from the dead dwell in you, he that raised up Christ from the dead shall also quicken your mortal bodies by His Spirit that dwelleth in you. Therefore, brethren, we are debtors, not to the flesh, to live after the flesh. For if ye live after the flesh, ye shall die: but if ye through the Spirit do mortify the deeds of the body, ye shall live" (Romans 8:10-13).

Even the body of a Christian is doomed to death if Jesus does not return in his lifetime. Nevertheless, the Christian has life because Christ lives in him. On a future day the body will be redeemed, but that time has not yet come. Our bodies are still under the curse. But the indwelling Spirit is our assurance that the curse will be removed. He is our guarantee that we shall receive a glorified body like Christ.

The Spirit living within us is our guarantee of a future bodily resurrection. Not only are we delivered from the law of sin, but we shall be delivered from the law of death. Complete redemption includes both body and soul.

Privileges bring obligations. This is true of spiritual privileges. We are debtors. We owe something. But we do not owe it to the flesh—our old carnal nature. We are obligated to Christ, and we can discharge our debt only by living "after the Spirit."

To live after the flesh is to court disaster. The flesh will clamor for attention, but by the power of the Spirit we can silence its voice. We must accept the

Lord's sovereignty over us, and be careful to obey Him always.

With Christ in the life there will be a walk in the Spirit. Christ lives in us through the Spirit just as surely as He lived physically among the disciples while He was on earth. It is a spiritual relationship now, but it is just as real. The Spirit has come in answer to Jesus' prayer to His Father. He is the "other Comforter" promised before our Saviour was crucified (John 14:16).

Paul says we must "mortify the deeds of the body." They must be constantly rejected. We must turn a deaf ear to the call of the flesh. This is not done in our own strength, but "through the Spirit."

This rejection of the flesh is a daily matter. It is part of our progressive sanctification. Christ does His part, and we must do ours.

ORPHANS NO MORE

"For as many as are led by the Spirit of God, they are the sons of God. For ye have not received the spirit of bondage again to fear; but ye have received the Spirit of adoption, whereby we cry, Abba, Father. The Spirit itself beareth witness with our spirit, that we are the children of God: and if children, then heirs; heirs of God, and joint-heirs with Christ, if so be that we suffer with him, that we may be also glorified together" (Romans 8:14-17).

Being led by the Spirit is a normal Christian life. It is the way we realize and prove our sonship. We are not spiritual orphans. We are children of God.

Many laws are passed every year for the purpose of protecting good men and punishing the bad. But righteousness cannot be legislated. Laws can be passed prohibiting drunken driving and dope addiction, but law does not change the drunkard or dope addict. When Christ comes into their hearts, however, they become "new creations."

Servants obey because they are subject to rules. Sons obey because they understand their father's will and want to please him. Christians are sons. They delight to do their Father's will.

Unbelievers may call on God in times of trouble, but only a son can truly pray, "Our Father." Not all men are children of God. The modernist teaching of the universal fatherhood of God and brotherhood of man is a doctrine straight from the pit of hell. Such teaching is unscriptural (John 8:44; 1 John 3:10).

But how wonderful is the assurance the believer has that he is God's son. Remember the word of Jesus to Mary Magdalene as she stood weeping at the tomb: "I ascend unto *my* Father, and *your* Father" (John 20:17). The Holy Spirit witnesses with our spirits to our sonship. He makes our position as sons real to us. If we yield to Him as He moves upon us we can assure our hearts that we are God's very own.

"Beloved, now are we the sons of God, and it doth not yet appear what we shall be: but we know that, when he shall appear we shall be like him, for we shall see him as he is" (1 John 3:2).

Paul points out another great privilege: Children are heirs. Because believers are children of God they are His heirs. They are joint-heirs with Christ. All things belong to Him, and we share in His eternal treasures.

Sometimes our joint-heirship with Christ involves suffering. But this only assures us of future glory. Sharing in His rejection by the world means sharing in His acceptance with the Father. There is all the difference in the world in simply suffering and suffering "with Him"—for His sake.

THE BEST IS YET TO COME

"For I reckon that the sufferings of this present time are not worthy to be compared with the glory which shall be revealed in us. For the earnest expectation of the creature waiteth for the manifestation of the sons of God. For the creature was made subject to vanity, not willingly, but by reason of him who hath subjected the same in hope; because the creature itself also shall be delivered from the bondage of corruption into the glorious liberty of the children of God. For we know that the whole creation groaneth and travaileth in pain together until now. And not only they, but ourselves also, which have the firstfruits of the Spirit, even we ourselves groan within ourselves, waiting for the adoption, to wit, the redemption of our body. For we are saved by hope: but hope that is seen is not hope: for what a man seeth, why doth he yet hope for? But if we hope for that we see not, then do we with patience wait for it" (Romans 8:18-25).

The hope of God's children is in the glorious return of Christ to earth. The victory of that coming day is so great that it makes all suffering seem minor.

When Jesus comes, God's sons will see their redemption completed. They will be "manifested"—unveiled. When that happens the whole "creation" will be redeemed. Sin affected even the animal and vegetable world, but this curse will be removed at the coming of Christ.

Paul says we "groan within ourselves" while we wait for this coming glory. The distressing conditions in our world today are a part of the groaning of the whole creation because of sin's terrible effects. But thank God, deliverance is on the way.

WE HAVE HELP

"Likewise the Spirit also helpeth our infirmities: for we know not what we should pray for as we ought: but the Spirit itself maketh intercession for us with groanings which cannot be uttered. And he that searcheth the hearts knoweth what is the mind of the Spirit, because he maketh intercession for the saints according to the will of God. And we know that all things work together for good to them that love God, to them who are the called according to his purpose. For whom he did foreknow, he also did predestinate to be conformed to the image of his Son, that he might be the firstborn among many brethren. Moreover, whom he did predestinate, them he also called: and whom he called, them he also justified: and whom he justified, them he also glorified" (Romans 8:26-30).

While we wait, we have the Holy Spirit's presence within. He, in sympathy with the groaning creation, prays through us. We have two intercessors: (1) The Lord Jesus at the Father's right hand, (2) the Holy Spirit, within us, here on earth.

OUR SUPPORT IS INVINCIBLE

"What shall we then say to these things? If God be for us, who can be against us? He that spared not his own Son, but delivered him up for us all, how shall he not with him also freely give us all things? Who shall lay any thing to the charge of God's elect? It is God that justifieth. Who is he that condemneth? It is Christ that died, yea, rather, that is risen again, who is even at the right hand of God, who also maketh intercession for us. Who shall separate us from the love of Christ? shall tribulation, or distress, or persecution, or famine, or nakedness, or peril, or sword? As it is written, For thy sake we are killed all the day long; we are accounted as sheep for the slaughter. Nay, in all these things we are more than conquerors through him that loved us. For I am persuaded, that neither death, nor life, nor angels, nor principalities, nor powers, nor things present, nor things to come, nor height, nor depth, nor any other creature, shall be able to separate us from the love of God, which is in Christ Jesus our Lord" (Romans 8:31-39).

No ultimate evil can befall God's children. Christ is "bringing many sons unto glory" (Hebrews 2:10). He will not lose them. They are His, and they will not be plucked out of His hand.

Paul asks six questions after he has emphasized God's side of man's redemption. The answers are given with positive confidence: Who would dare condemn us when the Judge of all the earth has acquitted us? Who would bring anything to our charge? God is for us! He was for us so much that He did not spare His only begotten Son. He was for us even though we were guilty, helpless, worthless, and sinful! Surely if God was for us to the extent of giving His Son He will bring us to final victory.

TEN

God Hasn't Forgotten Israel

CHAPTERS 9-11 OF THE EPISTLE TO THE ROMANS seem to depart from the trend of thought in the previous chapters. In fact, any reader will sense a definite break in moving from the end of Chapter 8 to the beginning of Chapter 12. The first eight chapters are doctrinal; the next three are dispensational; the last five are devotional.

In the doctrinal division Paul deals with the individual. In the dispensational division he discusses a nation and its destiny. He has been dealing with the church; now he deals with Israel.

Paul outlines God's relations with His chosen people in the past, present, and future. In the past Israel, as a nation, shunned God's favor and disregarded her opportunities. In the present Church Age Israel, as a nation, has rejected her Messiah. In the age to come Israel, as a nation, will accept the Messiah. Jesus. During His millennial reign she will enjoy the blessings promised in the Old Testament.

Paul is anxious to show that God's promises to the Church do not cancel His covenant with Israel. He will keep His Word to that nation. Israel is only temporarily set aside because of unbelief.

"I say the truth in Christ, I lie not, my conscience also bearing me witness in the Holy Ghost, that I have great heaviness and continual sorrow in my heart. For I could wish that myself were accursed from Christ for my brethren, my kinsmen according to the flesh, who are Israelites; to whom pertaineth the adoption, and the glory, and the covenants, and the giving of the law, and the service of God, and the promises; whose are the fathers, and of whom as concerning the flesh Christ came, who is over all, God blessed forever. Amen" (Romans 9:1-5).

There is a great difference between Israel and the Gentile nations. Israel is the covenant people, chosen of God. Someone has said that Israel is the only nation that is waterproof, fireproof, and indestructible in every way.

The Jew has been a problem to other nations. They have been able to absorb other nationalities rather quickly, but not the Jew. He has persisted through the centuries as a distinct ethnic group. He has retained his own religion, laws, and customs wherever he has gone. Many leaders of nations have tried to get rid of the Jews, but they have come and gone while the Jew remains.

Paul was a Christian, but he was also a Hebrew by nationality. He never lost his burden for his fellow Israelites. His concern for them was so deep that he would have borne their curse himself if it would mean their salvation.

GOD'S PURPOSE WILL STAND

"For this is the word of promise, At this time will I come, and Sarah shall have a son. And not only this; but when Rebecca also had conceived by one, even by our father Isaac, (for the children being not yet born, neither having done any good or evil, that the purpose of God according to election might stand, not of works, but of him that calleth;) it was said unto her, The elder shall serve the younger" (Romans 9:9-12).

The destiny of Israel has been shaped by their experience with two persons—Moses and Jesus. Moses was the one through whom God gave them His laws. He was their deliverer from Egyptian bondage. Jesus was their Messiah and King, but they rejected Him. Yet there will come a time when a portion of the nation will accept Him and He will return to earth to establish Israel as the world power God intended.

Israel came into being by a miracle. Abraham is the father of the race. Had God not intervened supernaturally Abraham would have had no descendants. But because the Lord gave Abraham and Sarah a son, Isaac, the covenant nation was begun and perpetuated.

Just as Israel had a miraculous beginning, she has had a miraculous preservation through the centuries. God's promise to Abraham will be fulfilled regardless of Jewish unbelief or Gentile oppression.

Paul answers the questions of sincere Jewish believers. They could not understand how their nation could be set aside for the Gentiles. Paul proves that the Word of God cannot fail. He makes a distinction between Abraham's natural offspring and his spiritual descendants. The Israelites God accepts are those of spiritual character.

God chose Isaac and not Ishmael. He chose Jacob and not Esau. Esau was the oldest son and would have been entitled to the blessings of the firstborn. But God had a different plan. In His sovereignty He set aside the elder in favor of the younger. This action rests upon "the purpose of God according to election."

God's promise to Abraham was based on His grace; not on Abraham's works. That promise has stood despite Israel's idolatry, rebellion, disobedience, and finally her rejection of Christ. Israel as a nation is still in unbelief, but this does not cancel the purpose of God. It will stand and triumph despite every human obstacle.

GOD'S SOVEREIGNTY

"What shall we say then? Is there unrighteousness with God? God forbid. For he saith to Moses, I will have mercy on whom I will have mercy, and I will have compassion on whom I will have compassion. So then it is not of him that willeth, nor of him that runneth, but of God that showeth mercy. . . . Therefore hath he mercy on whom he will have mercy, and whom he will he hardeneth. . . . What if God, willing to show his wrath and to make his power known, endured with much longsuffering the vessels of wrath fitted to destruction: and that he might make known the riches of his glory on the vessels of mercy, which he had afore prepared unto glory, even us, whom he hath called not of the Jews only, but also of the Gentiles? . . . What shall we say then? That the Gentiles, which followed not after righteousness, have attained to righteousness, even the righteousness which is of faith. But Israel, which followed after the law of righteousness, hath not attained to the law of righteousness. Wherefore? Because they sought it not by faith, but as it were by the works of the law. For they stumbled at that stumblingstone" (Romans 9:14-16,18, 22-24, 30-32).

As he does so often in Romans, Paul opens this portion with a question: "Is there unrighteousness with God?" The answer is a resounding, "God forbid!"

The questions of election and predestination are profound and controversial. They boggle the mind. No one really has the full answers. To natural reasoning these matters sometimes appear inconsistent. But man must recognize that God's thoughts are far above his. There are some things man must simply leave to God. This is where faith and trust enter the picture.

God does not create human beings for the purpose of condemning them. He is not responsible for the sinfulness of man. In Pharaoh's case God gave him repeated opportunities to repent. His heart was not hardened until he had rejected the light God gave him.

Ten times the Scripture speaks of Pharaoh's heart being hardened. He did not want God. He hardened his heart of his own volition. God then made him an example of His displeasure with sin. He made Pharaoh a picture of those who spurn His love and grace deliberately. His case is recorded in the Bible as an object lesson for all men.

Some people shrug off the matter of salvation by saying, "If I'm elected I'll go to heaven, and if I'm not I won't." But God says, "Whosoever" (John 3:16). He "is long-suffering to us-ward, not willing that any should perish, but that all should come to repentance" (2 Peter 3:9). God commands "all men every where to repent" (Acts 17:30).

Israel did not fail because of predestination. They failed because of their own choices. They stumbled over Christ.

Summing up Chapter 9 of his Epistle, Paul says

that a spiritual remnant, consisting of thousands of Jews, has accepted Jesus as Saviour, and therefore God's plan has not failed. These have been saved, and others have been rejected. This is in accordance with God's dealings in the past (Romans 9:6-13); is consistent with His justice (Romans 9:14-24); and is witnessed to by the Old Testament prophets (Romans 9:25-33).

Zeal Without Knowledge

"Brethren, my heart's desire and prayer to God for Israel is, that they might be saved. For I bear them record that they have a zeal of God, but not according to knowledge. For they, being ignorant of God's righteousness, and going about to establish their own righteousness, have not submitted themselves unto the righteousness of God. For Christ is the end of the law for righteousness to every one that believeth" (Romans 10:1-4).

Paul was deeply burdened over Israel's failure. Many times the Jews mistreated him, and even threatened his life; yet he still loved them.

The Jews had great religious zeal. They knew the Law. They performed its ceremonies with great exactness. They prided themselves on observing every small detail of God's ordinances. But their zeal was "not according to knowledge." It was misguided, and therefore missed the mark. The Jews had not properly interpreted the Law (Romans 10:3). They supposed that because they kept the letter of the Law they were automatically right with God. When Jesus came they felt no need of His offer of salvation. They answered Him, "We be Abraham's seed, and were never in bondage to any man" (John 8:33).

It is characteristic of all humans to try to win God's favor by good works. This desire is not limited to Jews. Everyone seems to feel that there is something he can "do" to earn salvation.

Paul says the Jews were "ignorant of God's righteausness." While ignoring His holiness, they worked feverishly to establish "their own righteousness." Here, again, is a familiar story. It is repeated all the time. Churches are full of people who think that because they have joined and gone through some religious ritual they are saved. They imagine that their good deeds are being stored up to be paraded before God at the judgment. In trusting their own righteousness they are ignoring God's plan of redemption.

"Christ is the end of the law for righteousness" because He is the only One who ever kept the Law perfectly. We can be righteous before God only by accepting the righteousness of Christ.

CONFESS AND BELIEVE

"That if thou shalt confess with thy mouth the Lord Jesus, and shalt believe in thine heart that God hath raised him from the dead, thou shalt be saved. For with the heart man believeth unto righteousness; and with the mouth confession is made unto salvation. . . . For whosoever shall call upon the name of the Lord shall be saved" (Romans 10:9,10,13).

God's great plan of righteousness is so wonderful and complete that man's efforts are excluded. Salvation can be received only by faith. Faith does not *win* a Saviour; it *accepts* the Saviour. Salvation is not limited to certain individuals or nations. It is for "whosoever shall call upon the name of the Lord."

Two parts of us are involved in salvation: Our heart and our mouth. The heart, of course, is the seat of our emotions and deepest feelings. It goes deeper than our thoughts. We do not accept Christ only with our mind. Saving faith is more than a mental assent. It goes to the deepest part of man's being. It involves both his will and his emotions. It is a complete trust and surrender.

But saving faith cannot be kept within ourselves. It must be confessed; announced to the world. If someone tries to hide his salvation he is likely to lose it. Confession is not a one-time act. We must confess Christ every day by the way we live. When opportunity is afforded we must witness to others about His saving power.

The thing God asks us to believe and confess is so simple. It is not a long list of rules and ceremonies to memorize. We must believe simply that Jesus died for our sins and rose from the dead for our justification.

"With the heart man believeth unto righteousness." This is where salvation starts—in the heart. Without this conviction in the heart any confession made with the mouth would be empty and mechanical. Some have "gone forward" in a church service and repeated answers to routine questions and imagined they were saved. But if there was not first a heart-deep faith and trust in Christ, all of those words were in vain.

"Whosoever" is one of the greatest words in the Bible. It is better than having your own name there. If your name were stated it would exclude everyone with a different name. But "whosoever" leaves out no one.

There is no prescribed way that we shall "call upon the name of the Lord." God deals with us as individuals, and we respond as individuals. Some experience great emotion; others do not. Some go through deep turmoil before they finally call. Others surrender quickly and quietly. The important thing is that we call in sincerity, in repentance, and in faith.

The Story Must Be Told

"How then shall they call on him in whom they have not believed? and how shall they believe in him of whom they have not heard? and how shall they hear without a preacher? . . . So then faith cometh by hearing, and hearing by the Word of God" (Romans 10:14,17).

Faith in the gospel depends on hearing it. This requires preaching. Preaching requires pastors, evangelists, and missionaries carrying the good news to all parts of the world.

But telling the story is not limited to those who preach from pulpits. It is the responsibility of every Christian. Some may object that they are timid and cannot speak. This is no excuse for not witnessing. We do not have to preach eloquent sermons to win souls. Our testimony may be self-conscious and awkward, but God will use it. The Holy Spirit will take the simplest words spoken for Christ and bring conviction to the unsaved heart.

It is a mistake to leave soul-winning to those we consider "full-time" workers. How can one pastor reach a community by himself? Are we guilty of thinking we can invite an evangelist for a meeting and push our job off on him? God deliver us from our laziness and lethargy!

Every member of the church must be involved in the great task of spreading the Good News. God has used angels to carry out many errands for Him. But

He does not use them to spread the gospel. His plan is for men who have been redeemed to tell others what Christ did for them. Laymen have contact with many whom the pastor can never meet. On the job, in the neighborhood, at the supermarket, the school, and a host of other places Christians meet people who need the gospel. Men must hear, God says, and it's from our mouths that the words must come.

ELEVEN

The Great Comeback

PAUL SAID SALVATION IS "TO THE JEW FIRST" (Romans 1:16). Has God forgotten this promise? "God forbid," replies the apostle.

The chosen people are only temporarily set aside. Their restoration will be the greatest "comeback" in history. When Christ gathers believers to himself at the end of this age God will turn again to Israel. His covenant promises shall be fulfilled without exception.

Many Old Testament passages refer to Israel's future. And that future is glorious. During this Church Age the nation is blinded spiritually; yet individual Jews are being saved. When Christ returns, all Israel shall be saved.

If God were to forget His' Word to Israel, what assurance would the rest of us have for our salvation? If He has cast off Israel might He not do the same with Gentile sinners? This is Paul's theme in Romans 11. It is very important to us.

This lesson becomes all the more vital as we consider it in the light of current events. Surely there are many signs that we are nearing what Paul calls "the fulness of the Gentiles." There are many evidences that God is turning His attention toward the chosen people and their land.

The land of Israel is the great stage on which the drama of this age's windup will be played. Israel is God's prophetic clock. Watch the clock very closely!

STILL A REMNANT

"I say then, Hath God cast away his people? God forbid. . . . God hath not cast away his people which He foreknew. Wot ye not what the Scripture saith of Elijah? how he maketh intercession to God against Israel, saying, Lord, they have killed thy prophets, and digged down thine altars; and I am left alone, and they seek my life. But what saith the answer of God unto him? I have reserved to myself seven thousand men, who have not bowed the knee to the image of Baal. Even so then at this present time also there is a remnant according to the election of grace" (Romans 11:1-5).

Paul himself was a great answer to the question, "Hath God cast away his people?" Paul was a Jew. He had been converted to Christ. That proved there is still a remnant. What happened to Paul will happen one day to the whole nation of Israel. No one was more spiritually blinded than Paul. He was a fierce hater of Christ and the church. He considered the new Christian religion blasphemous to the law of Moses. But on the Damascus road his spiritual eyes were opened. The Holy Spirit reached his heart with the Truth. He was saved, and began to proclaim the Christ he had once opposed so vehemently.

Before his conversion Paul was very zealous in his religion. But it was zeal without knowledge. He was trying to be righteous through the Law—just as the whole nation of Israel was doing.

Even the miraculous meeting Paul had with Christ

reminds us of the time the Saviour will appear to the Jews as their Messiah.

God has always had a faithful group. Elijah (Elias) thought he was all alone. But God revealed that 7,000 had not bowed their knees to Baal (vv. 3,4). As it was in Elijah's time, so now the elect are a remnant; a minority. When Jesus came, the nation as a whole rejected Him. They even asked that His blood be upon them. Yet there was a remnant that received Jesus.

The Book of Acts tells of thousands of Jews who became Christians. All of these were saved by grace, not works. They abandoned their efforts to be righteous by the Law, and trusted Christ. They became part of the Church.

The Church is not Jewish, nor national, nor earthly. The Church is "a new body," and it is a heavenly body. Those in the Church are not called Jews or Gentiles by the Lord. They are called "saints" (Romans 1:6,7; 1 Corinthians 1:2; Ephesians 1:1).

RICH THROUGH A FALL

"What then? Israel hath not obtained that which he seeketh for; but the election hath obtained it, and the rest were blinded. . . . I say then, Have they stumbled that they should fall? God forbid: but rather through their fall salvation is come unto the Gentiles, for to provoke them to jealousy. Now if the fall of them be the riches of the world, and the diminishing of them the riches of the Gentiles; how much more their fulness?" (Romans 11:7,11,12).

Election is of grace, not works, so while the remnant obtained grace the rest were blinded. God gave them the spirit of sleep in order to bring salvation to the Gentiles. This is revealed in Old Testament prophecies.

In outlining the history of the Jews, God said they would be scattered to all corners of the world. This was because of their spiritual blindness and rebellion against God. But along with these prophecies there are others speaking of Israel's future restoration and blessing. The Jewish race is a witness to the truth of God's holy Word. Their preservation is a miracle that can only be explained supernaturally. The rankest atheist cannot successfully argue against the fact that the history of the Jewish nation was foretold thousands of years ago.

Spiritually, Israel has fallen. But that fall has not been total because there has always been a believing remnant. The fall is not permanent. It is an example of God's overruling evil for good. "Through their fall, salvation is come unto the Gentiles." Spiritually the Gentiles have been made rich through the fall of the Jews. How much more, Paul says, will blessing come to the whole world when Israel comes back to God?

Since Israel was the nation chosen to receive God's laws, it would appear to the uninformed onlooker that their rejection of Christ doomed God's plan. Satan, of course, was the instigator of their refusal to accept Jesus as their Messiah. In this way he sought to block God's purposes, as he always does. But once again Satan is the defeated one. Israel is blind now, but their spiritual eyesight will be restored. They have fallen, but they shall rise. And during their time of spiritual poverty others have been partaking of the unsearchable riches of Christ.

God is never taken by surprise. He always has a

plan that overrules men's failures. Nowhere is this more clearly demonstrated than with Israel.

Even in the Jews' return to the land of Israel they have gone back in unbelief. Outwardly they appear no closer to accepting Christ than ever. But the words of the prophets will be fulfilled. A remnant will experience the visitation of God's Spirit. In answer to that remnant's cry, Christ will come to deliver them from their enemies.

BROKEN BRANCHES

"For if the casting away of them be the reconciling of the world, what shall the receiving of them be, but life from the dead? . . . And if some of the branches be broken off, and thou, being a wild olive tree, wert graffed in among them, and with them partakest of the root and fatness of the olive tree; boast not against the branches. . . . Because of unbelief they were broken off, and thou standest by faith. Be not highminded, but fear: for if God spared not the natural branches, take heed lest he also spare not thee" (Romans 11:15,17,18,20,21).

Through the tragedy of Israel's fall, salvation has been preached around the world to the Gentiles. A church is being built. Men of all nations have been delivered from sin. God has a great family of believers. All of this is the result of the spiritual blindness of the covenant people.

If all of this has happened because of Israel's fall, what glory awaits the whole world when Israel is restored. This is Paul's strong point in these verses.

The world's present turmoil is the prelude to that time of restoration. Israel is the center of much of the news today. The spotlight never turns away for long from that tiny nation. The whole world is concerned with Israel and its neighbors. This time of trouble is a necessary introduction to the time of Israel's spiritual comeback.

Paul uses the illustration of a tree and its branches. God's kingdom is like an olive tree, he says. Israel was the branches. The Gentiles were a wild olive tree. When Israel rejected Christ the branches of the olive tree were broken off. God filled the vacancy by grafting the wild olive branches into the tree. During this age the Gentiles are partaking of God's spiritual life —just as the branches partake of the life of the tree.

Paul warns the Gentile Christians not to boast over their position and glory over Israel's plight. "After all," he says, "you were just a wild tree. If the original branches had not been broken off, you wouldn't be in the tree at all." And he adds the warning that if God did not hesitate to break off the natural branches because of unbelief He certainly will not spare the wild branches if they fall into unbelief.

There is no room for boasting on the part of anyone over his spiritual condition. No one's standing with God is because of works. Were it not for God's grace we would all be lost—Jew and Gentile alike. Let us thank God that He loved the wild olive branches enough to graft them into the tree. We have only Him to praise for it.

THE COMING DELIVERER

"And they also, if they abide not still in unbelief, shall be graffed in, for God is able to graff them in again. . . . And so all Israel shall be saved, as it is written, There shall come out of Zion the Deliverer, and shall turn away ungodliness from Jacob: for this is my covenant unto them, when I shall take away their sins" (Romans 11:23,26,27).

As Paul states so clearly, the blessing of all nations

is linked with Israel's destiny. If Israel's rejection has brought such benefits to the world, who can fathom the blessings that will flow from their restoration.

Jesus is the Deliverer who shall come out of Zion. When He returns it will be a time when Israel needs a deliverer. Their plight will be worse than the Egyptian bondage from which they were delivered by Moses. God saw the suffering of His people then. He sent a deliverer. He will do so again at the end of this age.

Not only shall Christ deliver the Jews from their enemies. Greatest of all, He "shall turn away ungodliness from Jacob." There will be a spiritual revival in the nation. There will be the fulfillment of Ezekiel's vision of the valley of dry bones. At present the bones seem to have come together. There is a nation of Israel once more. But no spiritual life is present. This is yet to come. When it does, the Millennium will begin. During that period Israel will be the dominant nation of the world.

God says, "I will take away their sins" (v. 27). What a contrast between that coming day and the hour the Jews rejected Jesus and cried for Him to be crucified. They did not realize at that moment what consequences they were bringing on themselves. And they did not care. When Jesus returns as their Messiah He will cleanse the Jews of their sins. He will forgive their rejection of Him. It will be the great day of reconciliation. The natural branches of the tree will be grafted in again.

The fact that Jews are back in their own land today is the great miracle of our century. How long they were scattered everywhere! A return to Palestine seemed impossible. Then came Hitler and the horrible persecutions and slaughter. But out of this tragedy God brought good. It turned the hearts of Israel toward the Promised Land. It was the only home they had to go to. And they started going!

Praise God For It All!

"O the depth of the riches both of the wisdom and knowledge of God! how unsearchable are his judgments, and his ways past finding out!" (Romans 11: 33).

Just as the doctrinal portion of Romans climaxes in a glorious expression of worship to God (8:31-39), the dispensational portion (Chapters 9-11) is brought to a sublime conclusion in this chapter.

This section is pure praise, and is not given to argument. Yet it is the greatest argument of all. If we do not understand God's ways in His dealings with all men, Jew and Gentile, or even with the Church, it is because we are unable to comprehend the wisdom, knowledge, and ways of the Lord.

It is tragic that men are so willing to limit themselves to their own understanding. It takes childlike faith to trust in the wisdom of God. Many cannot humble themselves enough to admit that they do not know it all.

One of the worst dilemmas facing the world today is the Middle East problem. Diplomats are attacking it from every angle. Naturally the leaders of nations do not recognize the plan of God in all of this confusion. How thankful we can be that we have the light of the prophetic Word in times like these.

Keep Your Eyes Open!

The progressive aspects of Israel's return to the Holy Land are intensely significant to the Church. Jesus said very plainly that this Jewish restoration would be a sign of His second coming. Christians everywhere should pay close attention to the meaningful sermon that Israel is preaching to the church.

As Christians, let us be reminded that we must have a right attitude toward the Jews. They were the congregation of the Lord when there was no Christian church. From them we received our Saviour and the Scriptures. The first church was cradled in their nation, beginning in their holy city of Jerusalem. Every member of that church was a converted Jew. Those Jewish Christians left a greater impact for Christ upon the world than any succeeding generation up to the present time. And the greatest preacher, teacher, and missionary of this entire Church Age was Paul, a converted Pharisee. We owe so much to the Jew. Let us do what we can to win him to Christ.

The Jew will be the most prominent actor in the great events of the end time. No one can set dates for Christ's return, but we can know the season. The greatest signs of all are taking place in the Promised Land. Jesus commanded us to watch. Let's never let the dulling atmosphere of the world put our spiritual senses to sleep.

TWELVE

The Gospel in Shoe Leather

PAUL HAS BEEN DISCUSSING DOCTRINE, dispensations, and prophecy. Now he speaks of duty. Christianity is a practical religion. It fits us to be better men and women in this present world. If the gospel can't walk around in shoe leather there is something wrong with the one professing it.

Christians do not live in a vacuum. They rub shoulders with all kinds of people. They live in a world predominantly sinful. Believers cannot withdraw nor isolate themselves. They must cope with everyday problems and keep their faith in God.

Sound doctrine and practical Christian living go together. Strong beliefs make for strong character. When sound doctrine and rich experience are welded together there will be a life of happy service.

REASONABLE SERVICE

"I beseech you therefore, brethren, by the mercies of God, that ye present your bodies a living sacrifice, holy, acceptable unto God, which is your reasonable service" (Romans 12:1).

The Old Testament is full of sacrifices. Men constantly brought animals to kill on altars as offerings for their sins.

109

Such offerings are done away with in the New Testament. But sacrifice is still involved in our relation to God. The difference is that God is interested in living sacrifices; not dead ones. The sacrifice the Christian must bring is not an animal to kill. It is himself. He must present his body. Every day the Christian lives he must consider his life an offering to the Lord.

We make such a dedication because of God's mercies. This is the basis on which Paul "beseeches" the Romans. God does not stand over us with a club, saying, "Do this or I'll kill you." But His mercies are so great that it would be an ungrateful person who did not respond with all of his heart.

There is nothing unreasonable about God. He does not ask what we are unable to give. His requirement is our "reasonable service." This means "intelligent service." We do not serve God blindly. We do so with our minds as well as our hearts.

In presenting our bodies to the Lord as living sacrifices we must be sure that they are holy, Paul says. The Old Testament sacrifices had to be clean and unblemished. This is a picture of the kind of life God expects Christians to live in this present world—evil as it is.

Use the Right Pattern

"And be not conformed to this world: but be ye transformed by the renewing of your mind, that ye may prove what is that good, and acceptable, and perfect will of God" (Romans 12:2).

"Be not conformed" means literally "Be not cut according to the pattern." The shape of a manufactured article depends on the pattern from which it was made. The same is true of a life. Consciously or unconsciously everyone is using some kind of pattern to determine his way of life. Unfortunately many use the wrong patterns. Sin has great appeal. Often those who are the most godless seem to be prospering the most. Their life appears glamorous and attractive. Consequently many are led to pattern after them.

Today we constantly read of prominent people living together out of wedlock. We read and hear statements by such people ridiculing the marriage license as a scrap of paper. We observe the life-styles of some Hollywood stars, politicians, athletes, and others whose way of living is quite opposite to Biblical teaching. To a large segment of society these bad patterns become the ones they use. "Don't do it," Paul commanded. "Be not cut according to the pattern of this age. Instead of being conformed, be transformed."

Anything that displeases and dishonors God is conformity to the world. The Christian must strive to maintain God's viewpoint in relation to the world.

The expression "world" in this verse means the spirit which moves humans apart from the will of God. It means the spirit of selfishness, self-centeredness, lust, irreverence, greed, and submission to the devil.

The Christian is called on to be transformed (transfigured) by the renewing of his mind. When Jesus was transfigured before three of His disciples God's glory shown through Him, not upon Him. In like manner the indwelling Christ is to control our entire being so we will reflect His glory. This is the will of God. It is good and acceptable, and therefore perfect.

The "renewing of your mind" is a daily work. Our mind is renewed by keeping it full of the Word of God. It is renewed by keeping it submissive to the voice and will of the Holy Spirit. It is renewed by

111

keeping it focused on that which is good, holy, pure, and godly. Negatively our mind is renewed by rejecting that which would pollute our thinking and make it difficult to commune with God.

MANY, BUT ONE

"So we, being many, are one body in Christ, and every one members one of another" (Romans 12:5).

As Christians we are not isolated individuals. We are members of the true Church. Paul calls that Church Christ's body. The illustration of the body is a good one. A human body has all kinds of members —hands, feet, eyes, ears, etc. Each one is different, but all have a relation to the others. All must function properly if the body is to be at its best.

How true this is of Christians. Whether we like it or not, we have an influence on each other. We also have a responsibility to one another. If we allow our spirits to become carnal or sinful, it is like an infection striking a part of the body. It may be in the little finger, but the whole body will run a temperature.

As Christians we have a new nature. That new nature helps us get along with other people, and certainly with other Christians. Humility is a characteristic that should be easily detected in our lives. Paul says we should not overestimate our own importance. Whatever success may come our way is not due to our ability. It is God who has blessed us.

We are further implored to think soberly, so as to have sober judgment. Our ability is imparted according "to the measure of faith." In other words we are not to allow the possession of a spiritual talent to make us feel superior to other members of the church. Any spiritual power we may have comes as a gift of God.

Maintaining humility and avoiding pride involves the recognition of our dependence upon one another as fellow Christians. We need to appreciate the place and ministry which everyone performs.

Every part of the physical body is important. Each one has a definite function, and these functions are not interchangeable. If one is missing, the body is not up to par.

Christians are like these members of the body. We have "gifts differing according to the grace that is given us" (Romans 12:6). Seven of the gifts are enumerated in this 12th chapter. They are:

1. Prophecy—the gift of uttering God's will under the direct impulse of the Holy Spirit.

2. Ministry—administrative work, possibly the services as carried on by the deacons.

3. Teaching—to instruct in the truths of the Scripture.

4. Exhortation—to encourage, to entreat; an appeal to the will in contrast to teaching, which is an appeal to the mind.

5. Giving—sharing our substance readily and liberally.

6. Ruleth—referring to the elders and deacons.

7. Showeth mercy—engaging in practical deeds of helpfulness and kindness, and doing the same cheerfully.

FIGHT THE GOOD FIGHT!

"Be not overcome of evil, but overcome evil with good" (Romans 12:21).

This verse speaks of our relation to society. No one has to tell us that society in general is anti-God, anti-Christ, anti-purity, anti-morality, and anti-spiritual. This kind of atmosphere can overcome the Christian who does not resist it every day.

113

Here is where our individual responsibility enters the picture. God is for us. He wants us to win; not lose. He will do everything to equip us spiritually for the struggle. But on our part there must be determination, consecration, and endurance. It must be the purpose of our life that we are going to be overcomers, not overcome.

Paul says the way to overcome evil is with good. As formidable as sin's influence is, the power of the Holy Spirit is greater. We do not conquer the spirit of the age by running from it. We face it in the strength God gives us. We defeat it with the spiritual weapons He has placed at our disposal.

Christians have not been promised a favorable environment in which to live for God. Quite the contrary. The Bible is full of accounts of men and women who lived under the worst possible circumstances, yet rose above them. There are still believers doing it. Certainly we are in perilous times. But God has not withdrawn any of His grace from us. When the battle is upon us there will be strength from heaven.

There are accounts in the Bible of those who were overcome of evil, and these regrettable instances still take place. We must not get our eyes on those who have failed. We dare not assume that because they have been defeated we must follow the same path. We are the salt of the earth and the light of the world. Salt and light overcome their environment. Salt arrests decay. Light dispells darkness.

GOOD CITIZENS

"Let every soul be subject unto the higher powers. For there is no power but of God: the powers that be are ordained of God. . . . Render therefore to all their dues: tribute to whom tribute is due; custom to whom

114

custom; fear to whom fear; honor to whom honor"
(Romans 13:1,7).

The apostle speaks here of the Christian's responsibility as a citizen of his country. It is true that the
believer is a citizen of heaven. But he has not reached
heaven yet. While he is on the way he must live in
this world. He must be subject to laws, legislation,
and government.

A Christian citizen must walk very carefully. He
must not be among the number who deliberately flout
the laws of the land. He must not try to tear down
the rules of society. Paul says the Christian is to obey
the laws of the state. He is to obey the ruler, even
though he may be an ungodly man. It is the office he
is honoring, not the individual.

Both the church and the state are institutions of
God. He has ordained human government for man's
protection and progress. The church is a spiritual in-
stitution; the state a secular one. Both the saved and
the unsaved are under the laws of the state.

Believers must never be terrorists not anarchists. Unless governmental authority opposes God's commands
Christians must submit to it. If it does conflict with
one's loyalty to God then of course "we must obey
God rather than man" (Acts 5:29). But we must be
certain such a course of action is based on sincere
convictions. It must not be an effort to escape our
duty.

Paul emphasizes the God-appointed aspect of governmental authority. Five times in the first four verses of Romans 13 the phrase "of God" occurs. It indicates the origin of government. The origin is God's
authority. All government goes back to Him.

In His covenant with Noah (Genesis 9), God gave
the renewed earth into man's hand, and instituted

human government. God has never revoked that covenant. Therefore it is our duty to be good citizens of human government. Not only is this Paul's teaching; Peter also gives the same counsel (1 Peter 2:12-17).

God has ordained that government shall prescribe laws and then punish the offenders (vv. 3,4). If we obey the law we need have no fear of it.

Because government is of God we are to pay taxes (vv. 6,7) even if those taxes seem to be exorbitant. Paul tells us that the tax collectors "are God's ministers (servants), attending continually upon this very thing." The office, and not necessarily the man, is a ministry ordained by God.

It Won't Be Long

"The night is far spent, the day is at hand: let us therefore cast off the works of darkness, and let us put on the armor of light" (Romans 13:12).

Christians must live with a view to Christ's return. Romans 13:8-14 tells us how. We are to "owe no man anything, but . . . love." No conscientious Christian will assume more obligations than he can care for. God hates bad debts, and every Christian should hate them, too. Let every man's word be as good as his bond. Never dishonor the name of Christ by dishonest treatment of the creditor.

The first requirement for the office of deacon was that they should be "men of honest report." This preceded spiritual qualifications (Acts 6:3). Barnabas was "a good man" (Acts 11:24).

Christians are "to love one another." If a Christian loves his neighbor as himself he will take as much care of his neighbor's interests, his property, his good name, as he would of his own. He will never do any-

116

thing to harm him. He will thus fulfill God's law and man's law.

All of these things are to be done, and they are to be done now. The time is near when our Lord shall come to take us home. Every action should count for God and the glory of His Name, and we do not have much time left. It is high time to awaken out of the sleep of indifference and carelessness. The completion of our redemption is at hand. The night is far spent. Works of darkness must be cast off. We must put on "the armor of light."

"The day" Paul refers to here is the day of Christ's second coming. It is fitting to refer to this present age as "the night," for it is a time of great spiritual darkness. As students of the Word we know that darkness is coming to an end. And we pray, "Lord, keep us ready!"

THIRTEEN

How Free Is a Christian?

THE KEY VERSE OF THIS SECTION is 15:1: "We then that are strong ought to bear the infirmities of the weak, and not to please ourselves."

This immediately suggests that no Christian is free to live exactly as he pleases without regard to others. We are free from sin and Satanic bondage, but we are not free from spiritual obligations. We have liberty, but not license.

Every believer has a circle of influence. No matter how small it is, it touches others. Someone is watching us. They may rise or fall spiritually by our example. We may be an encouragement or a discouragement to those whose lives we contact.

Paul's teaching is directed especially to those "strong in faith." He gives instructions as to how they should walk before "him that is weak." It is undeniable that many Christians are weak. They are saved, but it doesn't take much to make them stumble. We must be careful that we are not the cause of their failure.

In this section of the epistle, Paul considers doubtful questions of conduct, open to dispute among Christians. Some very conscientious Jews were dis-

turbed about the eating of certain foods and the observance of feast days in the church at Rome. We
must remember that they had kept the Law for many
years before they found Christ. They were so scrup-
ulous that they were actually in bondage. Lifelong
teachings do not disappear quickly. There was great
emotional attachment to the Law and its ceremonies.
These Jewish Christians were not to be casually
slapped down by Gentile believers. There must be
mutual understanding. With their Jewish background
these "weak" brethren had not come to a full understanding of the grace of God.

Extremes have a way of infecting one's thoughts
and actions. The "strong" Christian is tempted to
think disparagingly of his "narrow-minded" friend.
The "weak" brother thinks the other man is very
worldly.

Paul instructs both to live peaceably. They are
brothers in Christ. Their differences of opinion must
not divide them. Each should treat the other with
love. They must avoid condemning one another, for
the Lord had received them all. There must be room
for liberty of conscience and for tolerance.

Two spiritual laws must be kept in proper balance
for all Christians. There is the law of liberty, which
permits Christians to engage in activities which,
though legitimate in themselves, may cause a question
mark in the minds of some. Then there is the law of
love, which moves the Christian to sacrifice his liberty
gladly rather than cause another to stumble.

DON'T BE A JUDGE

"Him that is weak in the faith receive ye but not to
doubtful disputations" (Romans 14:1).

This means that we are not to receive the weak

brother for the purpose of passing judgment on his opinions. We are to take him into our fellowship gladly without casting an eye of constant criticism in his direction.

There are certain essentials upon which all followers of Christ must agree. These are such truths as the inspiration and infallibility of the Bible; the Deity of Christ; the Virgin Birth; Christ's blood Atonement; the new birth; and many others. These are not negotiable. They are bedrock truths upon which the gospel rests. We cannot reject them and be saved.

However, there are other matters over which Christians disagree but which are not vital to salvation. They are not the great questions of doctrine, spirituality, or morality. They are the smaller details that arise from time to time. For example, some Christians believe it is wrong to drink coffee or eat pork, while others have no condemnation in these matters. Many other illustrations could be cited. Remember, we are not talking about things that are obviously wrong morally. If something is condemned in the Bible, that settles the matter. The subject before us is the matter of side issues over which there is room for differences of opinion.

In Chapter 13 Paul condemned those things that are immoral. But in Chapter 14, he warns against the danger of being too severe in questionable matters that are not expressly forbidden in Scripture.

Apparently these problems had arisen in the church at Rome. Otherwise Paul probably would not write about such matters. Some of the Christians, whom he calls "weak," were in bondage to regulations about certain foods and holy days. Some Gentile Christians, remembering the pagan customs from which they had been saved, believed in abstaining from meats (1

Timothy 4:3). Another group, influenced by Judaism, felt it was sinful to eat non-kosher foods. The vegetarians felt the meat-eaters were backsliders, while the other group even thought of excluding the vegetarians from fellowship.

Romans 14 and 1 Corinthians 8 are devoted to a burning question in the Early Church. Large quantities of meat were brought to the heathen temples for idol worship. What the heathen priests could not consume was sold to the people in the marketplaces. Since it was almost impossible to know if the meat purchased at the market had come from an idol's temple, the weak brethren found themselves unable to eat "a thing offered to an idol" (1 Corinthians 8:7). Therefore, to avoid defiling their consciences they confined their diet to vegetables.

This was a touchy question. The vegetarians were intensely sincere. Yet their convictions brought them into constant conflict with others who did not share their views.

His Glory in All Things

Notice how Paul deals with the problem. His wisdom was not purely natural; it was a gift of God. He does not put the strong in bondage, nor does he try to remove the scruples of the weak. Instead, he lays down principles which make it possible for both to live in peace with each other.

These same principles are applicable today in matters between Christians. As long as fundamental matters are not involved, Christians should live with harmonious consideration of each other even though they may disagree. The vegetarian has no right to judge his stronger brother. He who is "strong" is not to look with contempt on the abstainer. Paul gives us warning neither to despise nor judge a fellow believer. "God hath received him," and he will stand or fall before the Lord, whose servant he is.

Another problem, and one that is close to home in our day, is introduced in Romans 14:5. It is the observance of days. The Christian's Sunday is not a sabbath in the sense of the old covenant sabbath. The Christian does not follow the observance of the old covenant. But the first day of the week was set apart by the resurrection of our Lord Jesus. On that day He appeared to His disciples. The Christians observed the breaking of bread on the first day of the week (Acts 20:7). It was on that day they brought their offerings to the Lord (1 Corinthians 16:2). The first day of the week is the Lord's Day. It is sacred for His sake. We are not told exactly how to keep such a day. Our instructions are not as explicit as the rules for the Old Testament sabbath. But the Lord's Day is to be observed in worship.

When a question arises concerning something not specifically regulated by the Scriptures, Paul indicates that it must be a matter of personal conscience. "Let every man be fully persuaded in his own mind" (Romans 14:5).

Under the New Testament the standard of behavior is not "we must" or "we must not." But as we "put on the Lord Jesus Christ" (Romans 13:14) we are to do all things with one purpose—that it shall be to His glory. Our individual tastes and preferences are made subject to Christ. We can ask ourselves, "What would Jesus do?"

Over against verse 5 we have verse 7, which states, "for none of us liveth unto himself." In verse 5 we *think* for ourselves, but verse 7 tells us that we do not *live* for ourselves. The believer's actions are regulated with regard for the Lord.

The Bible tells us we are not our own. When it comes to life and its choices we cannot live just as we please. God's will and glory must be uppermost.

"It's Me, O Lord!"

"So then every one of us shall give account of himself to God" (Romans 14:12).

There is an old song, "Not the preacher, nor the deacon, but it's me, O Lord, standin' in the need of prayer." How wonderful it would be if we could spend more of our time watching ourselves and less time inspecting others.

We must answer to the Lord as individuals. We cannot question the Lord on that day, "But what about Brother Jones?" Brother Jones will answer for himself. So shall we.

Let us not judge others, but keep our own house in order. If we are truthful, all of us have to admit, "My greatest problem is me."

Don't Trip Your Brother

"Let us not therefore judge one another any more: but judge this rather, that no man put a stumblingblock or an occasion to fall in his brother's way. Let us therefore follow after the things which make for peace" (Romans 14:13,19).

There are limitations to our liberty. "We then that are strong ought to bear the infirmities of the weak, and not to please ourselves" (Romans 15:1). The strong Christian may be called upon to exercise great self-denial and sacrifice his liberty. He must do this for three reasons:

1. For the good of his weak brother. There must be no stumblingblocks put in his path. Things that

are harmless in themselves cease to be so when anyone sees harm in them (vv. 20,21). By insistence on his personal liberty the strong one may become a stumblingblock to another. His "meat" of self-gratification must never mean another's destruction.

2. For Jesus' sake. "Destroy not him with thy meat, for whom Christ died" (Romans 14:15). If Jesus gave His life for these, shouldn't the strong be willing to give up a small item of personal liberty for their sake and Jesus sake? Sometime you should take your concordance and check the number of times the expressions, "for Jesus' sake" and "for the Lord's sake" are used in the Bible.

3. For the good of the church. "For meat destroy not the work of God" (v. 20). We should not let "(our) good be evil spoken of" (v. 16). We must "follow after the things which make for peace, and things wherewith one may edify another" (v. 19).

How often the bickering of people has brought discredit to the work of God in a community. May we never tear down the work of God for the sake of personal gratification.

Paul points out two perils of liberty in the last two verses of this chapter. First, the strong brother is not to parade his liberties and insult the feelings of others (v. 22). If one is positive of his position he need never make a display of it. The man who is unsure of himself is usually the one who shows off his abilities.

Second, the weak brother has a peril, too (v. 23). If he, by the example of a stronger one, becomes bold enough to eat meat in spite of his conscience, he will be condemned. Because his action does not flow from faith he will walk in doubt and unhappiness.

124

If one is not sure about indulgences, amusements, and recreation, it is good to hesitate. Let conscience become clear by some decisive principle. And always be careful with the delicate faculty of conscience. If constantly pushed aside regarding trivial matters, it might become calloused on major matters later.

He Didn't Please Himself

"For even Christ pleased not himself; but, as it is written, The reproaches of them that reproached thee fell on me. . . . Wherefore receive ye one another, as Christ also received us to the glory of God" (Romans 15:3,7).

The Lord Jesus is our supreme example of self-sacrifice. His life teaches us to set aside personal privileges in order to help those who are weak. He "pleased not himself." Jesus spent His whole life in ministry to others. The multitudes thronged to Him. They took up His time, His strength, His ministry of teaching, healing, and blessing. He "came, not to be ministered unto, but to minister" (Matthew 20:28). As we are identified with Jesus our first concern will be to please Him. In turn we will strive to please our neighbor whenever it will promote his good and his Christian growth.

The Lord Jesus received us when we were sinners. He is very patient with us from day to day. He received the weaker brother. Can we refuse to be of the "same mind"? He is not only our Example; He will provide sufficient grace to enable us to imitate Him.

What a beautiful admonition: "Wherefore, receive ye one another." Those with opposite viewpoints in the church at Rome were doing the very reverse of this. They were clinging to the little groups and cliques that shared their ideas. A gap was developing between brethren, and much of it was caused by division over nonessentials.

"Christ received us," Paul reminds these folks. We were not perfect, but He received us anyway. We must do the same with our brothers and sisters in the Lord.

A BOLD LETTER

"And I myself also am persuaded of you, my brethren, that ye also are full of goodness, filled with all knowledge, able also to admonish one another. Nevertheless, brethren, I have written the more boldly unto you in some sort, as putting you in mind, because of the grace that is given to me of God, that I should be the minister of Jesus Christ to the Gentiles, ministering the gospel of God, that the offering up of the Gentiles might be acceptable, being sanctified by the Holy Ghost" (Romans 15:14-16).

On the official basis of his God-appointed office of apostle, Paul wrote the Romans "the more boldly." His ministry was strong and authoritative. He minced no words, and made no apologies for his teaching.

Christians through the centuries have been indebted to Paul for the profound, yet practical, teachings of the Roman epistle. His instructions about Christian liberty are as applicable today as when he wrote them. Times may change, but human nature does not.